CYBERCRIME CASES

IN A DECADE

The Malaysian Experience

RIZAL RAHMAN

ISBN-13: 978-1692537708
ISBN-10: 1692537709

Front cover image by Amazon.com, Inc.
Book Design by Amazon.com, Inc.

Paperback edition is available for purchase on Amazon:
https://www.amazon.com/CYBERCRIME-CASES-DECADE-MALAYSIAN-EXPERIENCE/dp/1692537709/

Kindle edition is available for purchase on Amazon:
https://www.amazon.com/CYBERCRIME-CASES-DECADE-MALAYSIAN-EXPERIENCE-ebook/dp/B07XSFT1R3

Associate Professor Dr. Rizal Rahman
Faculty of Law
Universiti Kebangsaan Malaysia
43600 Bangi
Selangor
www.researchgate.net/profile/Rizal_Rahman2

TABLE OF CONTENTS

ABBREVIATIONS

AMEJ	All Malaysia Electronic Judgements
AMLAFTA	Anti-Money Laundering, Anti-Terrorism Financing and Proceeds of Unlawful Activities Act
AMR	All Malaysia Reports
CLJ	Current Law Journal
COA	Court of Appeal
CMA	Communication and Multimedia Act
Daesh	A pejorative Arabic term used by the Malaysian authority to refer to the Islamic State Terrorist Group (IS)
HC	High Court
MLJ	Malayan Law Journal
MLJU	Malayan Law Journal Unreported
LNS	Legal Network Series
PP	Public Prosecutor

LIST OF CASES

INTRODUCTION

"Cybercrime" refers to a crime committed by using one or more computers. It should be emphasized here that the word "computer" here refers to any device that performs arithmetic, logic, storage and display functions, based on the definition given by section 2 of the Malaysian Computer Crimes Act 1997 (Act 563) and section 3 of the Malaysian Evidence Act 1950 (Act 56). In other words, as long as a device can be programmed to perform its functions using its artificial intelligence, the device is considered a computer. In today's era, it can be concluded that smartphones and tablets are included in the "computer" category.

In the Malaysian context, cybercrimes can be divided into two categories. The first category of cybercrimes relate to the security of computers including the program and data in them. Such crimes are dealt with by the Computer Crime Act 1997 as well as certain provisions of the Penal Code (Act 574), and to certain extent (also categorised as Financial Technology a.k.a. FinTech crimes) the Financial Services Act 2013 (Act 758), Anti-Money Laundering, Anti-Terrorism Financing and Proceeds of Unlawful Activities 2001 (Act 613) and Direct Sales And Anti-Pyramid Scheme Act 1993 (Act 500).

1

The second category of cybercrimes relate to content possession and communication from one computer to another. Such crimes are dealt with by the Communications and Multimedia Act 1998 (Act 588), certain provisions of the Penal Code, Sedition Act 1948 (Act 15), Film Censorship Act 2002 (Act 620), Anti-Fake News Act 2018 (Act 803) and to certain extent the Official Secrets Act 1972 (Act 88).

However, most of these cybercrime cases are heard only in the lower courts, namely the Magistrate Court and Sessions Court as these courts have original jurisdiction for such cases. The major legislative journals in Malaysia, including the Malayan Law Journal, Current Law Journal, All Malaysia Reports and databases like Westlaw (which also covers All Malaysia Electronic Judgements) and eLaw.my, are mainly focused on higher court judgments, namely the High Court, the Court of Appeal and the Federal Court. Although CLJ Law also publishes Sessions and Magistrates' Cases, it contains only selective judgments.

As for the judiciary based portals, the current relevant databases are the ejudgement portal (http://ejudgment.kehakiman.gov.my), and the Malaysian Judgement Portal (http://judgments.my), which was launched as a beta version on 17 April 2018. It is however quite difficult for the public to find a report on cybercrime cases from these portals, since the search string mechanisms are not user-friendly to them.

If we refer to books and journal articles, there are many publications on cybercrimes in Malaysia, but these publications do not highlight the decided cases in Malaysia but rather focus on reviews based on previous writings about cases in other countries. If we refer to the mass media, there are always media reports on such cases but most of the time they are only about statistics, criminal modus operandi and preventive mechanisms.

The first edition of the book i.e. "Cybercrime Cases in Malaysia" enlists the summary of selected decided cases on cybercrimes, mostly from the lower courts throughout Malaysia from 2009 to 2017. This edition contains more selected cases up until early 2019. Relevant citations for appeal cases, including those from the first instance cases which were mentioned in the first edition of the book, are also provided for further reference should the readers wish to read more about the grounds of judgement for those cases. An appendix is also provided should the readers wish to know more about the legal provisions referred to in the cases.

All cases have been indexed according to the dates of decision and relevant legislation for easier reference by the readers. Unless otherwise stated, the book adopts the *PP v (name of accused)* format, all accused persons were convicted and all sentences in the cases were ordered to run concurrently.

COMPUTER SYSTEM AND DATA SECURITY

Offences against Property under the Penal Code

PP v Ng Chee Wei [2019]

Ng Chee Wei, 23, a Grab driver was accused of concealing RM9000 belonging to Mohd. Sazali Saminan (victim) in his Maybank account which he allowed to be used in a scam. The act was committed via online transfer of RM900 and cash deposit of RM8100 to his bank account in May 2019.

The amount was transfered by the victim to Ng's bank account for the initial payment of a non-existent car fraudulently adverstised by two scammers on http://www.mudah.my. Ng was paid RM700 by the scammers.

Charge:
Section 424 Penal Code (2 charges)(pleaded guilty).

Decision of Shah Alam Magistrate Court (06/08/2019):
RM7500 fine.

PP v R. Jamunah [2019]

Jamunah, 23, a customer service officer was accused of stealing her sister's ATM card on 12 April 2019 and withdrawing RM400 from her account via Bank Simpanan Nasional ATM on 15 April 2019.

Charges:

Section 378 Penal Code (2 charges) (pleaded guilty).

Decision of Kuala Pilah Sessions Court (09/07/2019):

RM3,500 fine.

PP v Azizon Mat Nasan [2019]

Azizon Mat Nasan, 46, a university staff was accused of concealing RM5000 belonging to Nazihah Nasirudin (victim) in her bank account which she allowed to be used in a scam. The act was committed on 3 October 2018.

Charge:

Section 424 Penal Code (pleaded guilty).

Decision of Miri Magistrate Court (19/06/2019):

RM5000 fine.

PP v Karundendran Poopalan [2019]

Karundendran, 48, was accused of removing RM3500 belonging to another individual (victim) to his bank account which he allowed to be used in a scam. The acts were committed between 10 and 14 March 2017.

The victim earlier recieved a WhatsApp message from a scammer posing as a moneylender. Attracted by the loan package, the victim was then instructed to contact another scammer for the loan application of RM20,000. He then made a deposit payment of RM3,500 to Karundendran's bank accout for processing and legal fees. However, he did not receive further news about the matter, and his phone calls on the matter were also not picked up by the two scammers.

Charge:

Section 424 Penal Code (pleaded guilty).

Decision of Sibu Magistrate Court (19/06/2019):

30 months imprisonment.

PP v S. Prakash [2019]

Prakash, 39, an unemployed was accused of concealing RM4080 belonging to S. Arivukodi (victim) in his bank account which he allowed to be used in a scam. The act was committed between 25 February and 2 March 2017.

Charge:

Section 424 Penal Code (pleaded guilty).

Decision of Kuala Lumpur Magistrate Court (09/05/2019):

5 months imprisonment.

PP v Kasumawati Mohamad [2019]

Kasumawati, 45, a factory operator was accused of concealing RM12,800 belonging to Jelita Seis (victim) in her Maybank account which she allowed to be used in a parcel scam. The acts were committed in 4 occasions between 23 October and 5 November 2018.

Charges:

Section 424 Penal Code (4 charges) (pleaded guilty).

Decision of Port Dickson Magistrate Court (23/04/2019):

RM15,000 fine. Kasumawati failed to pay the fine and was ordered to serve imprisonment for 10 months.

PP v Chin Wei Yong [2019]

Chin, 26, a shop assistant was accused of concealing RM2050 belonging to an individual (victim) in his bank account which he allowed to be used in a scam. The act was committed on 6 May 2016.

The amount was transferred by the victim to Chin's bank account after receiving a phone call from a scammer who informed the victim that he had won a lucky draw of RM5000 from a telecommunication company, and thus he needed to pay a deposit of RM2050 to claim the prize money.

Charge:

Section 424 Penal Code (pleaded guilty).

Decision of Alor Gajah Magistrate Court (02/04/2019):

RM300 fine.

PP v Lam Ee Von [2019]

Lam, 36, a company director was accused of criminal breach of trust of company's money totalling RM9070.90. The amount was transferred to his Hong Leong Bank account in multiple transactions between 28 December 2016 and 17 March 2017.

Charges:

Section 409 Penal Code (2 charges).

Decision of Kuala Lumpur Sessions Court (06/03/2019):

Discharged and acquitted Lam since the prosecution failed to prove the case beyond reasonable doubt. The transactions were actually advance payment for "petty cash" and purchase of daily needs of the company.

PP v Muhammad Haziq Hilman Halim [2019]

Haziq, 20, a customer service officer was accused of concealing RM6000 belonging to Lai Wai Mun (victim) in his Ambank account to be used in a scam between 16 and 18 January 2018.

Charge:

Section 424 Penal Code (pleaded guilty).

Decision of Kuala Lumpur Magistrate Court (28/01/2019):

RM3000 fine.

| **PP v Sarimah binti Peri** |
| **Sarimah binti Peri v Pendakwa Raya [2019] MLJU 230** |

Sarimah was accused of receiving RM251,990 belonging to Koo Sai Lee (victim) in her CIMB account which was used in a scam. The acts were committed between 15 and 30 March 2016.

The victim earlier befriended via Facebook a scammer who fraudulently represented himself as a director at Shell oil and gas company. The deposit payments were made to "assist" him in settling his debt so that he would be receive USD4.25 million after the expiry of his contract with Shell.

Charge:

Section 424 Penal Code.

Decision of Klang Magistrate Court (30/06/2018):

2 years imprisonment.

Sarimah appealed against the decision of the Magistrate Court.

Decision of Shah Alam High Court (22/02/2019):

Allowed Sarimah's appeal on the ground that the magistrate had erred when she found that the prosecution had established a prima facie case.

PP v Lim Chau Ching [2019]

Lim, 34, a house builder was accused of receiving stolen money belonging to Azlina Abdul Aziz (victim) totalling RM5640 into his CIMB bank account between 21 and 22 December 2018.

The money was acquired after deceiving the victim about a housing loan. The victim earlier received a loan advertisement via a text message, and was asked to make a deposit payment.

Charges:

Section 411 Penal Code (2 charges) (pleaded guilty).

Decision of Kuala Terengganu Magistrate Court (18/02/2019):

RM2500 fine for each charge.

PP v Lim Ching Hai [2019]

Lim, 39, a masseur was accused of concealing RM149,737 belonging to Sim Teck Tan (victim) in his bank account which he allowed to be used in a scam between January to August 2010.

Charges:

Section 424 Penal Code (3 charges) (pleaded guilty).

Decision of Miri Magistrate Court (12/01/2019):

RM18,000 fine.

PP v Muhammad Lukmanhakiem Soekanto Pura [2019]

Lukmanhakiem, 20, was accused of concealing RM4000 belonging to Wong (victim) in his bank account which he allowed to be used in a scam in May 2018.

The victim earlier received a phone call from a scammer who informed him that his credit card was used in Genting Highlands and had total arrears of RM8,513.23. The scammer offered to assist the victim to update his personal information with the authorities, but the victim had to transfer all his money into Lukmanhakiem's bank account first. Although the victim was told the money would be refunded once the personal information had been updated, yet he heard no further news after the transfer.

Charge:

Section 424 Penal Code (pleaded guilty).

Decision of Sibu Magistrate Court (10/01/2019):

2 years imprisonment.

PP v Rosmaini [2018]

Rosmaini, 42, an Indonesian maid was accused of misappropriating RM800 from her employer's account via Maybank ATM in two transactions on 16 October 2018. The transactions were done using the victim's ATM card.

Charge:

Section 403 Penal Code (pleaded guilty).

Decision of Kuala Lumpur Magistrate Court (16/11/2018):

8 months imprisonment.

RM1600 fine.

PP v Tee Chiu Hang [2018]

Tee Chiu Hang, 29, a tile shop worker was accused of receiving stolen money totalling RM148,490 from Nor Faizah Othman (victim) into her bank account which she allowed to be used in Macau scam in multiple transactions between 21 April and 12 June 2017.

Tee earlier befriended two Nigerian scammers on Facebook, and surrendered her ATM card to them.

The victim also befriended the scammers on Facebook. She was informed that they wanted to send her valuables, but she needed to pay a deposit to Tee's account to release the items.

Charge:
Section 411 Penal Code (pleaded guilty).

Decision of Kuantan Magistrate Court (09/11/2018):
RM4000 fine.

PP v Shaarani Mohd Abas [2018]

Shaarani, 71, a retired assistant nurse was accused of receiving stolen money totalling RM3500 from Syazwani Othman (victim) into her bank account in multiple transactions between 2 and 4 September 2018. The money was acquired through parcel scam.

Shaarani earlier befriended a scammer on Facebook, and surrendered her ATM card to him.

The victim was earlier contacted by the two Nigerian scammers (one of them was the one befriended by Shaarani) who informed her that they wanted to purchase her motorcycle which was advertised online.

Charge:
Section 411 Penal Code (pleaded guilty).

Decision of Kuantan Magistrate Court (09/11/2018):
Released Shaarani on a good behaviour bond for a duration of 2 years.

PP v Mohammad Fahmi Shahrul Aruwar [2018]

Fahmi, 21, a welder was accused of concealing RM18,000 belonging to Bong Lan Chin (victim) in his CIMB bank account which he allowed to be used in a scam. The act was committed between 9 and 11 September 2018.

Fahmi earlier gave his bank card to his mother, and the card was then handed over to a third party who was a member of a scam syndicate.

Charge:
Section 424 Penal Code (pleaded guilty).

Decision of Petaling Jaya Magistrate Court (17/10/2018):
3 months imprisonment.

PP v Mohd Nadzrin Zaidel [2018]

Nadzrin, 23, an unemployed was accused of concealing RM10,479.48 belonging to a coffee shop owner (victim) in his Maybank account which he allowed to be used in Macau scam in multiple transactions on 17 January 2017.

The victim earlier received a text messafe from Nadzrin who warned him that his credit card had been used at Kuala Lumpur International Airport and Genting Highlands. The victim was advised to call the Central Bank using the phone number given in the message. When he made the call, another scammer posing as an officer from the Central Bank informed him that his personal information had been misused, unless he transferred his money to Nadzrin's bank account.However, after transferring RM10,479.48 to the account, the victim realised that he had been cheated.

Charges:

Section 424 Penal Code (2 charges) (pleaded guilty).

Decision of Sibu Magistrate Court (06/10/2018):

12 months imprisonment and RM3000 fine for the first charge.

18 months imprisonment and RM3500 fine for the second charge.

Nadzrin failed to pay the fine and was ordered to serve additional imprisonment for 6 months.

PP v Muhamad Akif Tajudin [2018]

Akif, 20, an unemployed was accused of concealing RM26,000 belonging to Turah Adiris (victim) in his CIMB bank account which he allowed to be used in a scam on 2 April 2018.

Akif earlier surrendered his ATM card to a scammer who offered to pay him RM150 for every card for bitcoin investment.

Charge:

Section 424 Penal Code (pleaded guilty).

Decision of Petaling Jaya Magistrate Court (05/09/2018):

RM6000 fine.

PP v G. Vani & Anor [2018]

G. Vani, 41, a bank officer was accused of allowing illegal transfers of RM40,600 and RM69,000 from a Maybank account on 12 January 2015.

Ristiyanti Mohd Isa, 38, a self-employed who was jointly tried with Vani was accused of assisting in concealing the above RM69,000 in her Standard Chartered bank account on the same date.

Charges:

Vani:

Section 409 Penal Code (2 charges).

Ristiyanti:

Section 414 Penal Code.

Decision of Kuala Lumpur Sessions Court (24/08/2018):

Vani:

6 years imprisonment and RM20,000 fine for the first charge.

5 years imprisonment and RM15,000 fine for the second charge.

Ristiyanti:

5 years imprisonment.

RM20,000 fine.

PP v Musa Md Dawi [2018]

Musa, 28, a clerk at the Special Warfare Training Centre was accused of dishonestly submitting 53 payment vouchers for travelling allowance and leave claims of 79 individuals, amounting to RM50,238.10 by falsifying the names of non-existent recipients.

RM46,281.10 was deposited to his bank accounts while the balance was transferred to accounts belonging to two other individuals in 2016.

Charges:

Section 403 Penal Code (79 charges).

Decision of Ayer Keroh Sessions Court (29/05/2018):

30 months imprisonment for each charge.

One stroke of cane for each charge.

The stroke of cane sentences were ordered to run consecutively.

PP v Sabariah binti Adam [2018]

Sabariah, 49, was accused of concealing RM9500 belonging to Normillah Binti Abdullah (victim) in her bank account which she allowed to be used in a parcel scam. The acts were committed in 2 occasions on 9 and 10 March 2015.

The victim earlier befriended a scammer posing as a pilot from Brunei on Facebook. She then received a phone call from another scammer posing as a freight carrier agent who notified her that the pilot had sent her a parcel. However, the parcel could not be delivered unless she paid the excess parcel fees and customs clearance fees since the parcel had been found to have contained undeclared dollar bill. The "agent" also threatened her that she could be charged with criminal offence if she refused to comply. At first she paid the amount as instructed, but when the "agent" contacted her again asking for more payment, she immediately lodged a police report.

Charges:

Section 414 Penal Code (2 charges).

Decision of Kuantan Magistrate Court (01/05/2018):

12 months imprisonment for each charge.

PP v Muhamad Sahrizal Ismail [2018]

Sahrizal, 35, a broadband installation contractor was accused of concealing RM20,000 belonging to Muhammad Yusri Mahat (victim) in his CIMB bank account which he allowed to be used in a scam. The act was committed on 27 March 2017.

The victim earlier received a phone call from a scammer posing as an officer from Affin Bank, notifying him that a new bank account was recently opened using his name in Penang. The "officer" also informed the victim that RM12,000 had been transferred from the account to another account owned by one "Lim Seng Siang" who was a dangerous drugs dealer and money launderer.

The victim then transferred RM20,000 to another bank account allegedly owned by an "auditor" in Putrajaya (Sahrizal's account) after receiving another phone call from a person posing as a police officer, warning him that the amount was needed for police investigation.

Charge:

Section 424 Penal Code (pleaded guilty).

Decision of Ayer Keroh Magistrate Court (14/03/2018):

14 months imprisonment.

PP v Khairil Najmi Ahmad Puzi [2018]

Khairil, 33, a driver was accused of removing RM9,798.38 belonging to Cheong Fook Ming (victim) to another CIMB bank account. The act was committed on 5 July 2017.

Charge:

Section 424 Penal Code (pleaded guilty).

Decision of Kuala Lumpur Magistrate Court (05/03/2018):

RM4000 fine.

PP v R. Muniandy [2018]

R. Muniandy, 37, a factory worker was accused of removing RM5500 belonging to Dzakaria Jantan (victim) to his CIMB bank account on 5 June 2017. Muniandy earlier surrendered his ATM card to a scammer for loan application, but the scammer later contacted the victim by posing as a moneylender. The victim was instructed to make insurance payments to secure the loan in multiple transactions to Muniandy's bank account.

Charge:

Section 424 Penal Code (pleaded guilty).

Decision of Kuala Lumpur Sessions Court (28/02/2018):

RM4000 fine.

PP v Rafidah Che Mat Zain @ Zainuddin [2018]

Rafidah, 42, a bank officer was accused of removing RM22,500 belonging to another individual (victim) to her bank account which she allowed to be used in a scam in multiple transactions. The acts were committed between June and July 2017.

Rafidah earlier surrendered her ATM card and pin number to a Nigerian scammer who later contacted the victim by posing as an FBI agent. The scammer informed the victim that her nude photo was about to be circulated on social media. To prevent that from happening, the victim was instructed to deposit RM12,500 to Rafidah's bank account. However, after she deposited the amount in multiple transactions, she was instructed to deposit another RM10,000 to the same account.

Charge:

Section 424 Penal Code (pleaded guilty).

Decision of Kuala Lumpur Magistrate Court (14/02/2018):

RM8000 fine.

PP v Mohamad Khusairie Fazni Aladin [2018]

Khusairie, 33, a Maybank officer was accused of criminal breach of trust of a client's account totalling RM53,870.64. The amount was transferred in multiple transactions to his account between April and June 2017.

Charges:

Section 409 Penal Code (103 charges)(pleaded guilty).

Decision of Limbang Magistrate Court (09/02/2018):

44 months imprisonment.

103 strokes of cane.

PP v Mohd Hafiszudin Rosdi [2018]

Hafiszudin, 30, a contractor was accused of concealing RM80,000 belonging to an individual (victim) in his Bank Islam bank account which he allowed to be used in a scam. The act was committed on 2 August 2017.

Charge:

Section 424 Penal Code (pleaded guilty).

Decision of Ampang Magistrate Court (06/02/2018):

15 months imprisonment.

PP v Nur Nirmal Manoj Kumar [2018]

Nirmal, 23, a housewife was accused of concealing RM900 belonging to Nor Hadhirah Abdul Hamid (victim) in her Bank Simpanan Nasional account which he allowed to be used in a scam. The act was committed on 20 March 2016.

The victim earlier agreed to purchase an iPhone 6 Plus which was advertised online for the price of RM1800. She was then instructed by Nirmal to make a deposit payment of RM900, and the balance to be paid after the delivery of the phone to her address. However, she later received a message asking for the balance payment to be paid before delivery, yet she was notified that she could cancel the purchase and her deposit money would be refunded. Although she decided to cancel the purchase, the deposit money was still not returned to her.

Charge:

Section 424 Penal Code (pleaded guilty).

Decision of Seremban Magistrate Court (05/02/2018):

RM1700 fine.

PP v Mohd Sazmey Mohamed Asri [2018]

Sazmey, 33, a labourer was accused of concealing RM3000 belonging to Mohd Nasir Ibrahim (victim) in his Bank Simpanan Nasional bank account which he allowed to be used in a scam on 14 June 2015.

The victim earlier agreed to purchase a Nissan Vannette vehicle from a scammer who fraudulently advertised the vehicle on http://www.mudah.my. He was then instructed by the scammer to make a deposit payment of the above amount to Sazmey's bank account to secure the booking. However, he received no further news on the matter after he made that deposit payment.

Charge:

Section 424 Penal Code (pleaded guilty).

Decision of Kota Bharu Magistrate Court (09/01/2018):

15 months imprisonment.

PP v Gollneer Roshandin [2017]

Gollneer, 61, was accused of receiving stolen money totalling RM37,800 belonging to Siti Hawa Hashim (victim) into her CIMB account in multiple transactions between 19 to 21 July 2017. The money was acquired through parcel scam.

The victim earlier befriended an Iranian scammer on Facebook. The scammer informed her that he wanted to give her a gift parcel containing a necklace, bracelet, ring and earring, plus a handbag and mobile phone, and a large sum of money in Iranian currency.

When she was later contacted by another scammer posing as a custom officer notifying her that she needed to pay a certain amount of money to collect the parcel, she immediately transfered the amount to Gollneer's bank account. However, she received no further news after the amount was paid.

Charges:
Section 411 Penal Code (10 charges) (pleaded guilty).

Decision of Sungai Petani Magistrate Court (26/12/2017):
RM1500 fine for each charge.

PP v Mariamah [2017]

Mariamah, 43, an Indonesian domestic cleaner was accused of stealing RM12,000 from her employer's account via CIMB ATM, Jalan Pegawai, Alor Setar in multiple transactions between 8 to 12 September 2016.

The transactions were done using an ATM card that she earlier stole from the victim, Sofiah Daud, 78.

Charges:

Section 378 Penal Code (8 charges) (pleaded guilty).

Decision of Alor Setar Sessions Court (15/11/2017):

24 months imprisonment.

RM8000 fine.

PP v Rose Suraya Ideris [2017]

Rose, 53, an unemployed was accused of concealing RM14,000 belonging to an individual (victim) in her bank account which she allowed to be used in a parcel scam. The acts were committed in multiple transactions on 8 September 2017.

The victim earlier befriended a scammer who fraudulently represented himself as a male person from United Kingdom and promised to give her a parcel gift from his country.

When the victim received a phone call on 8 September 2016 notifying her that a parcel was to be delivered to her, she agreed to pay RM14,000 "government tax" in advance so that the parcel could be couriered to her address. The money was transferred to the "courier's account" (Rose's account) in four transactions. However, the courier company asked for another transfer of RM70,000.

Charges:
Section 424 Penal Code (4 charges)(pleaded guilty).

Decision of Kuala Lumpur Magistrate Court (25/10/2017):
8 months imprisonment for the first charge.

7 months imprisonment for the second charge.

6 months imprisonment for the third charge.

9 months imprisonment for the fourth charge.

PP v Mohd Kamal Safinya [2017]

Kamal, 40, a lorry driver was accused of concealing RM797 belonging to Loke Bee Chin (victim) in his bank account which he allowed to be used in a scam. The act was committed on 15 July 2017.

Charge:

Section 424 Penal Code (pleaded guilty).

Decision of Kuala Lumpur Magistrate Court (02/10/2017):

RM1500 fine.

PP v Nurlina Mahamad Tajudin [2017]

Nurlina, 29, a bank cashier was accused of transferring RM14,000 belonging to Hesmiati Miring, a bank client to her Maybank account on 1 May 2017.

Charge:

Section 424 Penal Code (pleaded guilty).

Decision of Kota Kinabalu Magistrate Court (29/09/2017):

RM1500 fine.

PP v Nurliyana Mohd Sahari [2017]

Nurliyana, 34, was accused of concealing RM1000 belonging to Mohd Syafrin Affendi Abdullah (victim) in her bank account which she allowed to be used in a scam on 29 August 2017.

The victim earlier deposited the amount to Nurliyana's bank account as GST payment after being instructed by a scammer to enable the victim to make a loan of RM25,000.

Charge:

Section 424 Penal Code (pleaded guilty).

Decision of Seremban Magistrate Court (15/09/2017):

RM2000 fine.

PP v Mohd Nor Zaidi Borhan [2017]

Zaidi, 30, an unemployed was accused of concealing RM1100 belonging to Mohamad Alif Mohd Zuki (victim) in his bank account which he allowed to be used in a scam on 27 March 2015.

Charge:

Section 424 Penal Code (pleaded guilty).

Decision of Kota Bharu Magistrate Court (14/09/2017):

7 months imprisonment.

PP v Charles Sugumar a/l M. Karunnanithi [2017]

Charles, a tour driver, was accused of concealing RM36,300 belonging to Normila binti Abdul Hadi (victim) in his Maybank account which was used in a parcel scam. The acts were committed in 3 occasions between 17 and 18 November 2015.

The victim earlier befriended a scammer posing as a male from United Kingdom on Facebook. The scammer then informed the victim that he had received a job offer from Petronas in Kota Kinabalu and would bring his US$3 million cheque. Due to the large amount, he would not be able to convert it to cash without the victim's assistance. After receiving a phone call from another scammer posing as an officer from Standard Chartered Bank concerning the matter, the victim then transferred money to Charles's bank account so that the cheque could be cleared.

Charles was earlier requested by his customer (the scammer) to receive money on his behalf, since the customer's friend needed to transfer the money to him so that he could continue his tour in Malaysia.

Charges:

Section 424 Penal Code (3 charges).

Decision of Kota Bharu Magistrate Court (31/05/2017):

Discharged and acquitted Charles since the prosecution failed to prove the case beyond reasonable doubt.

The prosecution appealed against the decision of the court.

Decision of Kota Bharu High Court (07/09/2017):

Dismissed the appeal of the prosecution and retained the decision of the Magistrate Court.

PP v Syed Ahmad Nashrul Sayed Othman [2017]

Nashrul, 39, a chauffeur was accused of concealing RM500 belonging to an individual (victim) in his Hong Leong bank account which he allowed to be used in a scam on 9 August 2017.

The victim earlier agreed to make a personal loan of RM30,000 upon seeing a fraudulent advertisement by a scammer on Facebook. He then made a deposit payment of RM500 Nashrul's bank account as instructed to secure the loan.

Charge:

Section 424 Penal Code (pleaded guilty).

Decision of Seremban Magistrate Court (15/08/2017):

RM700 fine.

PP v Khairunnisa Ab Rahim [2017]

Khairunnisa, 26, a housewife was accused of concealing RM1700 belonging to Adelina Alies (victim) in her CIMB bank account in multiple transactions which she allowed to be used in a scam on 21 and 23 March 2017.

The victim earlier agreed to purchase a baby stroller fraudulently advertised online by a scammer. However, the stroller was not delivered to her after she made the purchase payment as instructed to Khairunnisa's bank account.

Charge:

Section 424 Penal Code (2 charges)(pleaded guilty).

Decision of Petaling Jaya Magistrate Court (10/08/2017):

4 months imprisonment for each charge.

PP v Minah Anak Nyangat [2017]

Minah, 38, was accused of removing RM6500 belonging to an individual (victim) to her Maybank account which she allowed to be used in a scam on 14 November 2016.

The victim earlier befriended a scammer who posed as an American by the name of Harding Scott on Facebook. The scammer told her that he would like to visit Malaysia and give her gifts and money. She later received a text message from him, informing her that she had to make some payment to Minah's bank account to release the gifts that he sent to her. However, after transferring RM6500 to the account, the gifts were still not delivered to her.

Charge:

Section 424 Penal Code (pleaded guilty).

Decision of Kuala Lumpur Sessions Court (25/07/2017):

5 months imprisonment.

PP v Jamalulhisham Jusoh [2017]

Jamalulhisham, 38, a security guard was accused of removing RM1300 belonging to Jolene Lim Shing Yu (victim) to his bank account which he allowed to be used in a scam on 16 May 2014.

The victim earlier transferred the above amount to Jamalulhisham account for the purchase of iPhone 5s fraudulently advertised on http://www.mudah.my.

Charge:

Section 424 Penal Code (pleaded guilty).

Decision of Kuala Lumpur Magistrate Court (24/06/2017):

3 months imprisonment.

PP v Tay Siao Leng [2017]

Tay, 28, an unemployed was accused of concealing RM RM15,000 belonging to Chong Tze Khiam (victim) in his bank account which he allowed to be used in a scam on 19 August 2016.

The victim earlier received a phone call from a scammer posing as a police Inspector who notified him that his son was detained with three other individuals for drug trafficking, punishable with death if convicted. He was instructed to make a payment of RM100,000 to release his son from police custody. The scammer agreed to reduce the amount to RM50,000 after being informed about the victim's financial constraints.

However, after depositing RM15,000 to Tay's bank account and the remaining RM10,000 and RM25,000 to other bank accounts under the name of other individuals, he discovered that his son had never been detained by the police.

Charge:
Section 424 Penal Code (pleaded guilty).

Decision of Miri Magistrate Court (04/03/2017):
4 months imprisonment.

PP v Lai Fook Fatt [2017]

Lai, 58, a company production manager was accused of illegally assisting in transferring RM49,000 belonging to another company manager to his own account on 14 December 2016.

The victim earlier received a phone call from Lai who accused him of using Lai's credit card in a premise in the Kuala Lumpur International Airport. The victim then transferred the above amount to Lai's bank account after receiving another phone call from a person posing as an officer from the Central Bank, warning him regarding the matter.

Charges:

Section 424 Penal Code (pleaded guilty).

Decision of Petaling Jaya Magistrate Court (22/02/2017):

9 months imprisonment.

PP v Mohamad Azmil Mohd Diah [2017]

Azmil, 24, an unemployed, was accused of cheating a fast-food outlet supervisor in relation to the sale of a smart phone (iPhone 6) which he advertised through WeChat in March 2016.

Charges:

Section 420 Penal Code (pleaded guilty).

Decision of Gua Musang Magistrate Court (02/02/2017):

3 years imprisonment.

5 strokes of cane.

PP v Jazrina Jaapar [2016]

Jazrina, 39, a freelance clerk was accused of concealing RM4150 belonging to Khairul Effendi Jasri (victim) in her CIMB bank account which she allowed to be used in a scam. The acts were committed in multiple transactions between 25 June and 11 July 2012.

The victim earlier agreed to purchase a Nikon camera advertised on http://www.mudah.my for RM4150, but after the amount was paid by installment to Jazrina's account in six transactions, the camera was still not delivered to him.

Charges:

Section 424 Penal Code (6 charges)(pleaded guilty).

Decision of Ampang Magistrate Court (29/11/2016):

7 months imprisonment.

PP v Mohamad Safari Ramidi [2016]

Safari, 40, a scrap metal collector was accused of concealing RM4000 belonging to Hoong Loong Famit (victim) in his CIMB bank account which he allowed to be used in a scam. The act was committed on 9 January 2012.

Charge:

Section 424 Penal Code (pleaded guilty).

Decision of Kuala Lumpur Magistrate Court (09/11/2016):

RM2000 fine.

PP v Siti Latifah Mohd. Said [2016]

Latifah, 29, a part-time computer application engineer was accused of masquerading as Khalisya Najwa in social media and deceiving a 28-year-old doctor until the victim handed over RM75,750 between October 7 and November 3, 2014. The money was purportedly to cover for the cost of their "upcoming marriage".

Charge:

Section 420 Penal Code (7 charges).

Decision of Ayer Keroh Magistrate Court (20/09/2016):

36 months imprisonment for each charge.

RM10,000 fine for the seventh charge.

PP v Jamaluddin Mohd Jamil [2016]

Jamaluddin, 34, a Maybank financial advisor was accused of criminal breach of trust of 33 client investment money totalling RM702,000. The amount was transferred to his Maybank account in multiple transactions between 2013 and June 2015.

Charges:

Section 409 Penal Code (56 charges)(pleaded guilty).

Decision of Petaling Jaya Sessions Court (31/05/2016):

30 years imprisonment.

24 strokes of cane.

PP v Nebolisa Olisa Hillary [2016]

Nebolisa, a Nigerian was accused of cheating a retiree via Facebook, after the latter befriended him who posed as an Arab-English male. When he informed her about his "financial problem", she transferred RM10,7950 to a Maybank account in multiple transactions on 7 December 2015 and between 8 to 15 December 2015.

Charges:

Section 420 Penal Code (2 charges) (pleaded guilty).

Decision of Batu Pahat Magistrate Court (11/02/2016):

18 months imprisonment and 2 strokes of cane for each charge.

PP v Mazrin Abd Aziz [2015]

Mazrin, 39, an unemployed, was accused of cheating a teacher and his wife in relation to the sale of a house which was not his property at a price of RM280,000 at http://www.mudah.my in 2014.

Charge:

Section 420 Penal Code (2 charges).

Decision of Kuala Lumpur Sessions Court:

2 years imprisonment and 2 strokes of cane for the first charge.

3 years imprisonment and 2 strokes of cane for the second charge.

PP v Mohd Fahzil Suherman [2015]

Fahzil, 26, was accused of misusing an ATM card belonging to Halimah Othman, 78, causing RM3800 losses to the victim at ATM Maybank Shell Timur Wawasan Enterprise, Sungai Besi on 3 June 2014. He was also accused of stealing an ATM card belonging to Noor Hazmi Hasbi, 27, from her car, and using the card to withdraw RM3000 from an ATM on 17 July 2014.

Charges:

Section 378 Penal Code (2 charges).

Decision of Kuala Lumpur Magistrate Court (09/10/2015):

7 months imprisonment, calculated from the date of arrest for the first charge.

7 months imprisonment for the second charge.

The sentences were ordered to run consecutively.

PP v Hamdan Abu Hussin [2014]

Hamdan, 27, an ATM technician was accused of stealing RM80,000 from a Maybank ATM at the lobby of the National Registration Department on 7 March 2013.

Charges:

Section 378 Penal Code.

Decision of Kuala Lumpur Sessions Court (16/12/2014):

1 month imprisonment.

RM20,000 fine.

PP v Erick Andrew Mbwambo [2014]

Erick, 19, a Tanzanian student from a private college was accused of concealing RM12,500 belonging to an individual in his Public bank, Hong Leong Bank and Affin bank accounts in multiple transactions between 27 and 30 June. The money was acquired through parcel scam. Erick was promised a reward of RM50 to RM100 for every transaction.

Charge:

Section 424 Penal Code (3 charges)(pleaded guilty).

Decision of Kuala Lumpur Magistrate Court (21/07/2014):

RM15,000 fine.

PP v Ramdan Mat Razak [2012]

Ramdan, 34, a bank operation manager was accused of criminal breach of trust of 6 Bank Islam client accounts totalling RM83,500. The amount was transferred in 95 transactions to three other accounts including one that belonged to his wife between 28 January and 20 March 2008.

Charges:

Section 409 Penal Code (95 charges)(pleaded guilty).

Decision of Shah Alam Sessions Court (02/02/2012):

2 years imprisonment for each charge.

2 strokes of cane.

RM20,000 fine.

PP v Peace Okotie [2009]

Okotie, 26, a Nigerian Business Management student from a private college was accused of cheating Md. Sayuti, 42, a public administrative officer via email about a $ 1 million (RM3.6 million) winning prize in 2008. She was also accused of residing in Malaysia with expired student visa.

Okotie informed the victim that she could manage the process of bringing in the Microsoft 2008 prize from the United Kingdom. The victim was deceived and transferred USD2750 (RM9969.85) to her account.

Charge:
Section 420 Penal Code (pleaded guilty).

Decision Kuala Lumpur Magistrate Court (24/03/2009):
16 months imprisonment.

Offences under the Computer Crimes Act 1997

PP v Sharil Fazrullah Shaib [2019]

Sharil, 24, was accused of withdrawing RM1480 from his mother's bank account via Bank Simpanan Nasional ATM in multiple transactions between 11 and 17 May 2019.

Charges:

Section 4(1) Computer Crimes Act (4 charges) (pleaded guilty).

Decision of Machang Magistrate Court (11/07/2019):

RM9000 fine.

PP v Che Mohd Affendi Azri Che Hussin [2018]

Affendi, 31, a lorry driver was accused of stealing a debit card from Ramli Ibrahim and withdrawing money from ATM in 3 transactions totalling RM12,600 on 2, 3 and 5 October 2017.

Charges:

Section 4(1)(a) Computer Crimes Act (3 charges) (pleaded guilty).

Decision of Kuala Terengganu Sessions Court (07/11/2018):

2 years imprisonment for each charge.

RM5000 fine for each charge. The sentences for the 1st and 3rd charge were ordered to run concurrently.

PP v Mohd Zukainiel Yusof [2018]

Zukainiel, 39, was accused of withdrawing RM12,150 from a bank account owned by Ismail Mohd in multiple transactions between 22 January to 14 February 2017. He earlier posed as a bank staff responsible in managing umrah and pilgrimage package before he managed to deceive the victim to hand over his ATM card and password for the payment of the non-existent package.

Charges:

Section 4(1)(a) Computer Crimes Act (11 charges) (pleaded guilty).

Decision of Kuala Terengganu Sessions Court (20/09/2018):

1 year and 6 months consecutive imprisonment for each charge.

PP v Lau Jia Wen [2018]

Lau, 23, an electronics and furniture company employee was accused of modifying the advertised price of iPhone 7 Plus from RM4299 to RM4.99 on the website of the company without authority with the intention to cheat on 22 July 2017.

Charges:

Section 5(1) Computer Crimes Act.

Decision of Kuala Lumpur Sessions Court (16/05/2018):

RM3000 fine.

PP v Chee Han Hing & Anor [2018]

Chee Han Hing, 38, a mobile phone dealer and his employee, Tan Shi Wei, 26, were accused of unauthorised access to Multi-Channel Portal and unauthorised modification to its content on 27 February 2016. The acts were committed for the purpose of 18 fraudulent sim cards registration without verifying the end user's information as required by DiGi Telecommunications Sdn Bhd.

Charges:

Section 5(1) Computer Crimes Act (18 charges) (pleaded guilty).

Decision of Sepang Sessions Court (29/03/2018):

RM3000 for each charge (first accused).
RM1000 for each charge (second accused).

PP v Hasimah binti Aziz [2018]

Hasimah was accused of allowing an unauthorised access to her Maybank account to assist the commission of parcel scam against Saliza bin Jam on on 13 and 14 July 2017.

Charge:

Section 4(1)(b) Computer Crimes Act.

Decision of Kuala Lumpur Sessions Court (02/03/2018):

Discharged and acquitted Hasimah as there was no prima facie case.

PP v Zuraidah Abdullah [2017]

Zuraidah, 31, a cashier at Sport Planet Odeon Walk, Jalan Tuanku Abdul Rahman was accused of unauthorised multiple ATM withdrawals amounting to RM10,000 and an unauthorised debit payment of RM184 to purchase shoes at the same store on 1 October 2017. The transactions were done using an ATM card unintentionally left by Malkeet Kaur, 40 a customer at the store.

Charges:

Section 4(1)(a) Computer Crimes Act (pleaded guilty).

Decision of Kuala Lumpur Sessions Court (19/10/2017):

RM6000 fine.

| **PP v Kangaie Agilan a/l Jammany v PP [2015]** |
| **Kangaie Agilan a/l Jammany v PP [2017] MLJU 1647** |

Kangaie, 27, a pre-flight officer at AirAsia Regional Reservation Control (RRC) was accused of multiples unauthorised modifications of AirAsia flight booking system by changing the flight schedules in the system so that his family members and friends could benefit from the low prices. The acts were committed between 20 March 2009 to 22 August 2010 using an ID and password entrusted to him by a superior officer.

Charges:
Section 5(1) Computer Crimes Act (148 charges).

Decision of Shah Alam Sessions Court (02/09/2015):
5 years imprisonment for each charge.

He appealed against the decision.

Decision of Shah Alam High Court (27/02/2017):
Dismissed the appeal.

PP v Vishnu Devarajan [2016] AMEJ 1729

Vishnu, 39, a former Executive at Astro Radio Sdn Bhd, was accused of committing a series of unauthorized access and modifications to the Astro server located at Technology Park Malaysia on 18, 19 and 21 October 2012.

Charges:

Section 3 Computer Crimes Act (10 charges).
Section 5 Computer Crimes Act (26 charges).

Decision of the Sessions Court (03/07/2015):

Discharged and acquitted Vishnu after hearing the argument of the prosecution and Vishnu, upon receiving an Application Notice which was supported by Vishnu" s Affidavit dated 19 May 2015.

The prosecution appealed against the decision of the court.

Decision of Kuala Lumpur High Court (13/04/2016):

Dismissed the appeal of the prosecution and retained the decision of the Sessions Court.

PP v Roslan Mohamed Som and Anor [2014]
Roslan bin Mohamad Som and Anor v PP [2016] AMEJ 1392
(HC)

Roslan, 51, a clerk at the Pilgrims Fund Board (TH), was accused of receiving a bribe of RM6750 from Shamsudin Ibrahim to allow a group of pilgrims to skip the queue so they could perform their pilgrimage in 2010. Afizul, 38, a senior analyst at the Pilgrims Fund Board, was accused of assisting Roslan by committing unauthorised access to TH database and keying in their records. Shamsudin Ibrahim was the agent who managed the group of pilgrims.

Charges:

Section 17(a) Malaysian Anti Corruption Commission Act (Roslan).
Section 5(1) Computer Crimes Act (Afizul) (3 charges).

Decision of Kuala Lumpur Sessions Court (04/05/2014):

4 years imprisonment and RM40,000 fine (Roslan).
3 years imprisonment and RM20,000 fine for each charge (Afizul).

They appealed to the High Court.

Decision of Kuala Lumpur High Court (30/06/2016):

Dismissed the appeal by Afizul and Roslan, retained conviction and sentence.

PP v Hasliani Hashim [2016]

Hasliani, the account manager for D'Herbs health and beauty products, was accused of withdrawing money from a bank account owned by Datuk Aliff Syukri (her employer) via ATM in 3 transactions which amounted to RM4500 without his knowledge.

Charge:

Section 4(1)(a) Computer Crimes Act (3 charges).

Decision of Ampang Magistrate Court (27/01/2016):

Discharged and acquitted Hasliani after the DPP informed the Court that he had received an instruction from the Senior DPP for the charges to be withdrawn at the request of the victim.

PP v Abdul Malik Awang Abd Hamid [2014]

Abdul Malik, 35, a courthouse clerk was accused of accessing a password belonging to an account assistant to cancel the issuance of a payment receipt for a RM10,000 fine at the Kota Kinabalu Courthouse Complex payment counter on 28 February 2012.

Charge:

Section 4(1)(a) Computer Crimes Act (pleaded guilty).

Decision of Kota Kinabalu Sessions Court (08/07/2014):

1 day imprisonment and RM15,000 fine.

PP v Tung Lun Tak [2014]

Tung Lun Tak, 44, a dealer, was accused of supplying and selling online 47 units of devices i.e. 5 units of High Power Signal King, 7 units of Sinmax and 35 units of WiFiSky not certified by SIRIM, to infiltrate other users" broadband systems, on 22 October 2013.

Charge:

Section 239(1) CMA.

Decision of Kuala Lumpur Sessions Court (28/04/2014):

RM15,000 fine or 1 year imprisonment.

PP v Nor Shafarilla Ahmad Tahir [2011]

Shafarilla, 27, was accused of dishonestly withdrawing money from a bank account owned by her friend Nurul Haireena Isnin via ATM in 4 transactions which amounted to RM1090.

Charge:

Section 4(1)(a) Computer Crimes Act (4 charges) (pleaded guilty).

Decision of Kuala Lumpur Magistrate Court (09/11/2011):

RM2000 fine each for the first and second charge,

RM1500 fine each for the third and forth charge.

She only managed to pay RM3500, and thus was sent for 7 months imprisonment for failure to pay the remaining RM3500.

PP v Sosaya Carraso and Ors [2011]

Sosaya Carraso Jose Wilfredo, 57; Henry Fernando Carrascal Carlin, 44; and Nicanor Edgar Areche Aquipa, 44, citizens of Peru, were accused of deceiving Ma Kalthum Salleh, 38, and withdrawing her money (RM3500) via ATM (Maybank Besut) on September 2010.

While the victim was withdrawing her money at the ATM, her shoulder was tapped by one of the accused who showed her some cash notes on the floor. She then bent down and picked up the money.

When she was done with the withdrawal and took out her card from the ATM, she noticed that the card looked different. After checking with the bank, it was revealed that RM3500 from her account had been withdrawn before the bank managed to cancel the usage of the card.

Charge:

Section 4(1)(a) Computer Crimes Act read with Section 34 Penal Code (pleaded guilty).

Decision of Kuala Terengganu Sessions Court:

18 months imprisonment.

PP v Muhammad Rashid Narayanan [2010]

Rashid, 28, a contractor, was accused of trespassing the Finance Minister's e-mail account at http://www.treasury.gov.my and then using the email, ybmk@treasury.gov.my to impersonate the Finance Minister by sending e-mails to 2 officers of the Ministry of Finance to obtain a project tender or business opportunity. However, the two officers were not deceived.

The offence was committed at the Putrajaya Finance Ministry Complex at 9.42am, 12 April 2010.

Charge:

Section 4(1)(a) Computer Crimes Act (2 charges) (pleaded guilty).

Decision of Putrajaya Sessions Court (03/05/2010):

RM6000 fine for each charge.

Multiple Offences under the Penal Code and Computer Crimes Act 1997

PP v Rose Hanida bt Long [2016]
Rose Hanida bt Long v PP [2017] MLJU 1212

Rose Hanida, 36, a secretary to the Head of Corporate Banking Department at OCBC Bank was accused of 13 series of unauthorised access using ID and password belonging to the Department Head. The acts were committed to cheat the OCBC Bank Finance Department by submitting false financial claims, causing the department to approve and deposit RM348,294.81 to her account in 160 transactions, between January 2010 to December 2013.

Charges:

Section 4(1)(a) Computer Crimes Act (13 charges).

Section 420 Penal Code (13 charges).

Decision of Kuala Lumpur Sessions Court (30/08/2016):

1 year imprisonment for each charge under section 4(1)(a).

RM15,000 fine for each charge under section 4(1)(a).

4 years imprisonment for each charge under section 420.

RM 5,000 fine for each charge under section 420.

She appealed against the sentences.

Decision of Kuala Lumpur High Court (20/07/2017):

Dismissed the appeal and ordered her sentences to be increased:

6 years imprisonments for each charge.

RM260,000 fine for all 26 charges.

PP v Ahmad Zakri Raman [2017]

Zakri, 31, an Assistant Registrar at Malacca National Registration Department (JPN) was accused of receiving a RM88,000 bribes for the purpose of issuing MyKad to 22 Sulu people of the Philippines between April 2015 to March 2016.

He was also accused of hacking the National Population Records Information System (SIREN) by altering the citizenship status of all the same individuals between March 2014 to April 2016.

Charges:

Section 161 Penal Code (17 charges).

Section 5 Computer Crimes Act (15 charges) (pleaded guilty).

Decision of Ayer Keroh Sessions Court (02/03/2017):

3 years imprisonment for each charge under Section 161 Penal Code.

7 years imprisonment for each charge under Section 5 Computer Crimes Act 1997 (concurrent sentence which will be executed upon serving the above sentence under Section 161 Penal Code).

PP v Nur Shila Kanan and Anor [2015]
Basheer Ahmad Maula Sahul Hameed and Anor v PP [2016] 6 CLJ 422 (HC)

Nur Shila, 34, a HSBC bank officer, and her husband Basheer, 34, a mechanic, were accused of transferring and withdrawing RM85,180 from 3 passengers and 1 crew who were the victims of MH370 tragedy.

The act was committed by using the victims' debit cards at the ATM machine, transferring money using unauthorized internet access, stealing money via manual money transfer and submitting fake debit card application document as genuine.

Charges:

Section 378, 417 and 471 Penal Code.

Section 4(1)(a) Computer Crimes Act.

Nur Shila: 12 charges.

Basheer: 4 charges.

They pleaded guilty.

Decision of Kuala Lumpur Sessions Court (21/05/2015):

Nur Shila:

10 months to 6 years imprisonment for each charge

(28 years and 4 months imprisonment).

Basheer:

2 years imprisonment and 1 stroke of cane for the first charge.

2 years imprisonment and 1 stroke of cane for the second charge.

3 years imprisonment and 1 stroke of cane for the third charge.

4 years imprisonment and 1 stroke of cane for the fourth charge.

They appealed to retract their plea of guilt.

<u>Decision of Kuala Lumpur High Court (16/05/2016):</u>

Dismissed the appeal.

Ordered Basheer's sentence for the fourth charge to be increased to 6 years imprisonment, 2 strokes of cane and RM8000 fine.

Ordered Nur Shila's sentence for the 12th charge to be increased to 7 years and RM7000 fine.

Both of them had to undergo only 6 years imprisonment (Basheer) and 8 years imprisonment (Shila) since the court ordered the sentence to run concurrently.

PP v Sahaslina Mat Yazid [2016]

Sahaslina, 29, an administrative assistant at the Road Transport Department (RTD), was accused of criminal breach of trust of motor vehicle license fees amounting to RM14,452 at the counter of the Vehicle Licensing Division at Level 1, RTD Terengganu between June 1 and October 15, 2014.

She was also accused of committing unauthorized modification by revoking the motor vehicle license transaction.

Charges:

Section 409 Penal Code (Sessions Court).

Section 5(1) Computer Crimes Act (25 charges in the Magistrate Court).

Pleaded guilty to the charge at the Sessions Court.

Decision of Kuala Terengganu Sessions Court:

3 years imprisonment and RM15,000 fine.

Sentence began from the date of arrest i.e. 30 December 2015.

PP v Irwan Samsu [2013]

Irwan, 28, was accused of stealing a Public Bank ATM card belonging to Mardiannah Sardi, 38, at Salon Ketty Studio on May 8, 2013. He was also accused of fraudulently withdrawing the victim's money in a series of transactions amounting to RM12,800 using the victim's ATM card without her knowledge.

Irwan obtained the pin number of the ATM card after telling the victim that he needed the pin number of the so-called lost card for investigation at the police station.

Charges:

Section 380 Penal Code.

Section 4(1)(a) Computer Crimes Act 1997 (14 charges).

Decision of Tawau Magistrate Court:

4 months imprisonment and RM2000 fine for the charge under the Penal Code.

2 months imprisonment and RM2000 fine for each of the 14 charges under the Computer Crimes Act.

PP v Mohd. Afdzal Rizal Rashid and Anor [2011]

Afzal, 31, contract officer at Selangor Land Office was accused of modifying the details of registered owners on a computerized document of title number 28191 and 28192 with the intention of causing loss to them, at the Selangor Land office on July 30, 2003. Gan Kiat Bend*, 47, an unlicensed land broker abetted him.

Afdzal used the computer in the office for the purpose of securing access to the computerized Land Registry System program with the intention of causing loss, as well as improperly altering the data in it.

Charges:

Section 467 Penal Code (2 charges).

Section 4(1)(a) Computer Crimes Act.

Section 5(1) Computer Crimes Act (alternative charge).

Decision of Shah Alam Sessions Court (25/01/2011):

Discharged and acquitted Afdzal since there was no prima facie case.

*In a case relating to the land lots (*PP v Gan Kiat Bend and Anor [2011] 8 CLJ 951*), Gan Kiat Bend and Ismail Husin (also a unlicensed land broker) were sentenced to 5 years imprisonment and RM1 million fine by the Sessions Court on December 23, 2010 after being found guilty of 16 charges of money laundering amounting to almost RM5 million between November 19, 2003 and January 5, 2004.

They appealed to the High Court but the Court dismissed their appeal on March 10, 2017.

Offences under the Anti-Money Laundering, Anti-Terrorism Financing and Proceeds of Unlawful Activities 2001, Financial Services Act 2013 and Direct Sales and Anti-Pyramid Scheme Act 1993

> ### PP v MBI Marketing Sdn Bhd (MBI) and Mface International Sdn Bhd (Mface) [2018]

MFace, MBI, Mface director Kau Fong Seng, 35, and MBI director Teow Wooi Huat, 52, were accused of issuing electronic payments unrecognised by Bank Negara Malaysia (BNM), promoting pyramid scheme and involvement in money laundering between 3 June 2012 and 17 March 2018.

Charges:

Mface:

Section 27B Direct Sales and Anti-Pyramid Scheme Act 1993.

Section 24(1) of the Payment System Act 2003*.

Kau:

Section 4(1) Amlafta.

MBI:

Section 24(1) Payment System Act 2003.

Teow:

Section 24(1) Payment System Act 2003.

All accused pleaded guilty.

Decision of Ampang Sessions Court (16/08/2018):

Mface:

RM7 million fine for the charge under the Direct Sales and Anti-Pyramid Scheme Act 1993.

RM2.5 million fine for the charge under the Payment System Act 2003.

Kau:

RM5 million fine.

MBI:

RM2.5 million fine.

Teow:

RM3 million fine.

*The Payment System Act was repealed and replaced by the Financial Services Act in 2013.

PP v Wong Pei Hur [2012] 5 LNS 52
Wong Pei Hur v PP [2013] (HC)
Wong Pei Hur v PP [2015] (COA)

Wong Pei Hur, 39, a multi-level marketing operator of AB Fund was accused of illegal internet investment activities involving an amount of more than RM2 million.

Charges:

Section 25(1) Banking and Financial Institutions Act (BAFIA)* 1989 (2 charges).
Section 4(1) AMLAFTA (20 charges).

The Sessions Court discharged the accused from the offences under BAFIA upon hearing the preliminary objection by the accused that the charges were defective.

The prosecution applied for the decision on the discharge to be reviewed by the High Court. Although the High Court dismissed the application, yet the Court of Appeal upon appeal from the prosecution decided on 27 October 2011 that the charges were not defective, and thus ordered for the accused to be tried for the offences under BAFIA.

Decision of Kuala Lumpur Sessions Court (23/04/2012):

4 years imprisonment for each charge under BAFIA.

A total of 16 years and 3 months imprisonment for charges under AMLAFTA.

The sentences under AMLAFTA were ordered to run concurrently, thus the accused needed to serve only 2 years imprisonment for the 20 AMLAFTA offences. However, the sentences under AMLAFTA and BAFIA were ordered to run consecutively.

The accused appealed against his conviction to the High Court.

Decision of the High Court (30/08/2013):

Dismissed the appeal.

Decision of the Court of Appeal (10/06/2015):

Allowed the appeal and quashed conviction and sentence by the Sessions Court.

*BAFIA was repealed and replaced by the Financial Services Act in 2013.

PP v Phazaluddin bin Abu [2010]

Phazaluddin, 49, a business man was accused of operating an online investment scam without holding a fund manager's licence. The investigations by the Malaysian Securities Commission revealed that he had raised RM65 million from 52,000 investors in 2007 via the website www.danafutures.com, which claimed to be an asset management and investment group focusing on business and fund management.

He was also accused of taking part in money laundering activities involving a sum of RM1.3 million.

Charges:

Section 15A(1) Securities Industry Act 1983*.

Section 4(1) AMLATFA (3 charges).

Decision of Kuala Lumpur Sessions Court (09/07/2010):

4 years imprisonment for the charge under the Securities Industry Act.

2 years imprisonment for each charges under AMLAFTA.

Phazaluddin is the first person in Malaysia to be convicted of operating an illegal online investment scam.

* The Securities Industry Act was repealed and replaced by the Capital Market and Services Act [Act 671] in 2007.

CONTENT POSSESSION AND COMMUNICATION BETWEEN COMPUTERS

Offences under the Communication and Multimedia Act 1998

PP v Syahzan Amir Endut [2019]

Syahzan, 41, an employee of Universiti Utara Malaysia was accused of disseminating an obscene photo of his ex-girlfriend via MMS on 28 March 2015.

Charge:

Section 233(1)(a) CMA.

Decision of Kulim Sessions Court (26/09/2018):

RM15000 fine.

The prosecution appealed against the sentence.

Decision of Alor Setar High Court(22/07/2019):

Dismissed the appeal by the prosecution.

PP v Sharil Mohd Sarif [2019]

Sharil, 36, a gardener was accused of insulting the Yang di-Pertuan Agong and the Malay Rulers on Facebook using the profile name of "Sharil Chain" on 13 March 2019.

Charge:

Section 233(2) CMA (pleaded guilty).

Decision of Kuala Lumpur Sessions Court (26/04/2019):

2 months imprisonment.

PP v Mohd Yazid Kong Abdullah [2019]

Yazid, 52, was accused of posting an offensive statement against Islam and Prophet Muhammad on Facebook, using the profile name of "Yazid Kong" on 28 February 2019.

Charge:

Section 233(1)(a) CMA.

Decision of Kuala Lumpur Sessions Court (11/03/2019):

7 months imprisonment.

RM10,000 fine.

PP v Sirirat Pichetwanich [2019]

Sirirat, 33, a Thailand citizen was accused of posting a nude photo of her friend on Facebook using the profile name of "IamthebonusIamthebonusiamthebonus" on 23 August 2018. She did that after allegedly finding out that her friend had an affair with her husband.

Charge:

Section 233(1)(a) CMA (pleaded guilty).

Decision of Petaling Jaya Sessions Court (07/03/2019):

9 months imprisonment.

PP v Mohd Fahmi Redza bin Mohd Zarin [2018]
Mohd Fahmi Redza bin Mohd Zarin v PP [2017] MLJU 516 (HC)
Mohd Fahmi Redza bin Mohd Zarin v PP [2018] (HC)

Fahmi, 39, a graphic designer was accused of posting a clown drawing depicting the Prime Minister on Instagram using the profile name of "kuasasiswa" on 31 January 2016.

He was also accused of posting a false warning poster allegedly issued by the Malaysian Communication and Multimedia on Facebook, with the same clown drawing, on 8 February 2016.

Charges:

Section 233(1)(a) CMA (2 charges).

He faced the trial for the first charge before Ipoh Sessions Court, and the second charge before Kuala Lumpur High Court.

Fahmi applied to the High Court to quash the charges on the ground that section 233 Communication and Multimedia Act violates Article 8 and 10(2)(a) of the Federal Constitution.

Decision of Kuala Lumpur High Court (29/03/2017):

Referred the matter to the Federal Court.

Decision of the Federal Court (31/10/2017):

Remitted the case to the Sessions Court, after ruling that there was a procedural error in the constitutional challenge against the charges.

Decision of Ipoh Sessions Court (20/02/2018):

1 month imprisonment.

RM30,000 fine.

Decision of Kuala Lumpur Sessions Court (11/10/2018):

Discharged and acquitted.

Fahmi appealed against the decision of Ipoh Sessions Court.

Decision of Ipoh High Court (12/11/2018)

Dismissed the appeal against conviction, but substituted the sentence with RM10,000 fine.

PP v Mohd. Hannan Ibrahim [2018]

Hannan, 27, a fish delivery man was accused of insulting the death of two policemen in a road accident on "Komuniti Kuantan" Facebook page. The comment ".. padan muka polis segelintir jahat hahahahahahaha hahahah" (serves the police right some are bad), was posted on 23 October 2018.

Charge:

Section 233(1)(a) CMA (pleaded guilty).

Decision of Kuantan Sessions Court (26/10/2018):

6 months imprisonment.

PP v KiniTV, Steven Gan Diong Keng and J. Premesh Chandran [2018]

KiniTV, an internet video portal and its directors, Steven, 56, and Premesh, 49, were accused of posting offensive videos of former Batu Kawan Umno Vice Chief Datuk Seri Khairuddin Abu Hassan criticizing the Attorney General. The videos with the title "Khairuddin: Apandi Ali not fit to be AG, he should quit immediately" and "Khairuddin: Apandi Ali tidak layak jadi AG" were uploaded to KiniTV on 27 July 2016.

Charges:

Section 233(1)(a) CMA.

Section 244(1) CMA.

The accused applied for the charges to be referred to the High Court on the ground that they violate Article 5, 8 and 10 of the Federal Constitution, but the Kuala Lumpur Sessions Court denied their application on 13 February 2018.

Decision of Kuala Lumpur Sessions Court (20/09/2018):

Discharged and acquitted all the accused persons after the prosecution withdrew the charges against them.

PP v Syarul Ema Rena Abu Samah [2018]

Syarul Ema, 37, a building construction consultant was accused of insulting the Prime Minister via Facebook with the profile "Ratu Naga", regarding the Trans-Pacific Partnership Agreement on 6 October 2015.

Charge:

Section 233(1)(a) CMA.

Decision of Sepang Sessions Court (25/07/2018):

Discharged and acquitted Syarul Eme after the prosecution withdrew the charge against her.

PP v R. Sivarasa [2018]

Sivarasa, 62, a lawyer was accused of posting a fake front cover of Time magazine containing the photo of the then Prime Minister Datuk Seri Najib Razak on his Facebook page using the profile name of "Sivarasa Rasiah" on 22 and 23 March 2016.

Charge:

Section 233(1)(a) CMA (2 charges).

Sivarasa applied to the High Court to quash the charge on the ground that section 233 Communication and Multimedia Act violates Article 8 and 10(2)(a) of the Federal Constitution.

Decision of Kuala Lumpur High Court (24/01/2018):

Dismissed the application on the ground that section 233(1)(a) and 233(a) CMA are not in violation of Article 8 and 10(2)(a) of the Federal Constitution.

Decision of Kuala Lumpur Sessions Court (28/06/2018):

Discharged and acquitted Sivarasa after the prosecution withdrew the charges against him.

PP v Mohammad Khairul Abidin Abdul Rahim [2018]

Khairul, 34, a restaurant manager was accused of posting obscene photos of his ex-girlfriend to a blog on 16 June, 4 July and 7 July 2015.

Charge:

Section 233(1)(a) CMA (3 charges) (pleaded guilty).

Decision of Kuala Terengganu Sessions Court (17/04/2018):

3 years imprisonment.

PP v Azizan Ahmad [2018]

Azizan, 64, a retiree was accused of posting false content on Facebook, regarding a report that a shipping container from Spain contained a mixed storage of frozen pork and lamb. The post was made on 20 July 2017.

Charge:

Section 233(1)(a) CMA (pleaded guilty).

Decision of Kuala Lumpur Sessions Court (03/05/2018):

RM2000 fine.

PP v Nik Azmi Nik Mustapha [2018]

Nik Azmi, 40, a Police Officer was accused of posting a false content about the Prime Minister and Deputy Prime Minister on Facebook on 12 December 2016. The content was posted using the profile name of "Nik Azmi Nik Mustapha".

Charge:
Section 233(1)(a) CMA.

Decision of Kuala Lumpur Sessions Court (19/04/2018):
Discharged and acquitted after the prosecution failed to prove the case prima facie.

PP v Mohd Asrul Alwin Mohd Yusoff [2018]
PP v Ainin Syazwani Che Mat Noordin [2018]

Asrul, 32, a factory engineers and Ainin, 22, a polytechnic graduate, were both accused of posting false content on Facebook, regarding a report that a shipping container from Spain contained a mixed storage of frozen pork and lamb, on 20 and 21 July 2017.

Charge:
Section 233(1)(a) CMA (pleaded guilty).

Decision of Kuala Lumpur Sessions Court (13/04/2018):
RM3000 fine.

PP v Roslan Ahmad [2018]
PP v Maizura Abu Bakar [2018]

Roslan, 54, a retired teacher and Maizura, 54, an herbs entrepreneur, were both accused of posting false content on Facebook, regarding a report that a shipping container from Spain contained a mixed storage of frozen pork and lamb. The posts were made on 19 July 2017.

Charge:

Section 233(1)(a) CMA (pleaded guilty).

Decision of Kuala Lumpur Sessions Court (09/03/2018):

RM2000 fine.

PP v Shamsiah Samsuddin [2018]

Shamsiah, 44, a housewife was accused of insulting the Yang di-Pertuan Agong, Sultan Muhammad V via Facebook with the profile "Tengku Cik Puan Muda Shamsiah" on 25 April 2017.

Charge:

Section 233(1)(a) CMA (pleaded guilty).

Decision of Kota Bharu Sessions Court (25/03/2018):

8 months imprisonment.

PP v Muhammad Amirul Helmy [2018]

Amirul, 24, a crane operator was accused of insulting the Prime Minister in a comment to a video of the latter singing "Shalala" at a karaoke session with President of the Philippines. The video was posted to his Facebook page using the profile name of "Amirul Helmy" on 18 November 2016.

Charge:

Section 233(1)(a) CMA (pleaded guilty).

Decision of Kuala Lumpur Cyber Court (16/02/2018):

RM4000 fine.

PP v Azhar Mamat [2018]

Azhar, 45, a retailer was accused of insulting the Prime Minister and the Attorney General on his Facebook page with the profile "Azhar Mamat" on 21 and 27 July 2016. He was also accused of posting a false content on Facebook on 29 July 2016. One post contained a doctored image of the Prime Minister in police remand attire.

Charges:

Section 233(1)(a) CMA (4 charges) (pleaded guilty).

Decision of Kuala Lumpur Sessions Court (09/02/2018):

RM5000 fine for each charge.

PP v Yeu Bang Keng [2018]

Yeu (popularly known as Beng Kor), 50, an activist and organiser for 'Sarawak for Sarawakians (S4S) movement was accused of non-cooperation with the police in their investigation against his comment on his Facebook page. He refused to supply the police with his id and password on 15 May 2017.

He was alleged to have labelled the then Chief Minister Datuk Sri Adenan Satem as "bodoh" (idiot) regarding matters related to the Malaysia Agreement 1963 on his Facebook page "Sarawak Keluar Malaysia 2021".

Charge:

Section 249 CMA.

Decision of Sibu Sessions Court (15/01/2018):

Discharged and acquitted after the prosecution failed to prove the case prima facie.

PP v Datuk Zaid Ibrahim [2018]

Zaid, 67, a politician was accused of posting an offensive article "'Rally Behind Tun Dr Mahathir Mohamad" against the Prime Minister to his blog http://www.zaid.my on 3 September 2015. The article was based originally a speech delivered on 2 September 2015 at Selangor Royal Club.

Charge:

Section 233(1)(a) CMA.

Decision of Kuala Lumpur Sessions Court (11/01/2018):

Discharged and acquitted after the prosecution failed to prove the case prima facie.

PP v Mohd Shahriman Shahir Omar [2017]

Shahriman, 39, an unemployed was accused of posting an offensive comment against the Yang di-Pertuan Agong and Prime Minister on his Facebook page using the profile name of "Mohd Shahriman Omar" on 11 October 2016.

Charge:

Section 233(1)(a) CMA (pleaded guilty).

Decision of Kuala Lumpur Cyber Court (14/12/2017):

RM10,000 fine.

PP v Muhammad Naim Zelkifle (2017)

Naim, 21, was accused of posting a false comment on N9RPTER Facebook page, alleging that police officers asked for bribe from the public during a road block. The comment was posted on 6 September 2017.

Charge:

Section 233(1)(a) CMA (pleaded guilty).

Decision of Bahau Magistrate Court (10/11/2017):

RM2000 fine.

PP v Mohamed Mustafa Shaikh Ismail (2017)

Mustafa, 25, an NGO leader was accused of posting a video of Port Dickson primary school headmaster and a parent on Facebook, with a false caption alleging that the headmaster was trying to bribe the parent after the parent was beaten by a teacher from the school. The video was posted on 17 July 2017.

Charge:

Section 233(1)(a) CMA (pleaded guilty).

Decision of Seremban Sessions Court (25/10/2017):

RM8000 fine or 4 months imprisonment.

PP v Muhammad Farhan Burhan [2017]

Farhan, 19, a school student was accused of insulting the Sultan of Perak by posting "Sultan Perak pun bodoh" (Sultan of Perak is stupid too) via his Twitter account @farhaleigh on 13 October 2017.

Charge:

Section 233(1)(a) CMA (pleaded guilty).

Decision of Ipoh Magistrate Court (19/10/2017):

RM5000 fine or 3 months imprisonment.

PP v Sheikh Noor Affandi bin Sh. Ab. Ghani [2017]

Affandi, 40, was accused of posting a comment on his Facebook page: "Yahoo! Dah mampus Sultan Negeri Kedah Darul Aman" which insulted the demise of the late Sultan of Kedah, Almarhum Tuanku Abdul Halim Muadzam Shah.

Charge:

Section 233(1)(a) CMA(pleaded guilty).

Decision of Kuala Lumpur Cyber Court (27/09/2017):

RM5000 fine.

7 days imprisonment.

PP v Mohamad Hamizan Ghazali [2017]

Hamizan, 24, a factory operator was accused of uploading an offensive cartoon which insulted the Prime Minister on his Facebook page "Ieyzan Ghazali" on 20 and 22 October 2016.

Charge:

Section 233(1)(a) CMA (pleaded guilty).

Decision of Petaling Jaya Magistrate Court (19/09/2017):

4 months imprisonment.

PP v Lee How Kim [2017]

Lee How Kim, 26, a contractor was accused of uploading photographs of his traffic summons and tinted windscreen of his car and initiating defamatory comments against the Royal Malaysian Police (PDRM) on his Facebook page "Raymond Lee" on 19 July 2017. He earlier received a summon by the traffic division for pasting something on the window screen of his car.

Charge:

Section 233(1)(a) CMA (pleaded guilty).

Decision of Petaling Jaya Magistrate Court (18/09/2017):

RM4000 fine.

PP v Mohd Basyir Abu Bakar [2017]

Basyir, 27, a businessman was accused of sending an obscene SMS to a female teacher on 1 to 4 March 2016.

Charge:

Section 233(1)(a) CMA (10 charges) (pleaded guilty).

Decision of Kuala Terengganu Sessions Court (18/09/2017):

3 months imprisonment for each charge.

PP v Kamarzaman Mustafa [2017]

Kamarzaman, 56, a Telekom Malaysia retiree was accused of posting a false comment related to the recent seizure by the Department of Malaysian Quarantine and Inspection Service (Maqis) of four 30-tonne containers storing halal and non-halal frozen meat together on his Facebook page "YB Kamarzaman" on 19 July 2017.

Charge:

Section 233(1)(a) CMA (pleaded guilty).

Decision of Kuala Lumpur Sessions Court (11/09/2017):

RM5000 fine.

PP v Muhammad Zaidi Abdullah [2017]

Zaidi, 40, a a shoe shop assistant was accused of uploading a doctored photo of the Prime Minister with scantily clad women on his Facebook page "Zaidi Zura" on 3, 5 and 6 December 2016.

Charge:

Section 233(1)(a) CMA (pleaded guilty).

Decision of Kuala Lumpur Sessions Court (20/07/2017):

1 day imprisonment and RM3500 fine.

PP v Norimran Kusairie Ibrahim [2017]

Norimran, 39, was accused of sending a menacing content with the intent to extort a woman on 13 May 2016.

Charge:

Section 233(1)(a) CMA (pleaded guilty).

Decision of Taiping Sessions Court (20/11/2017):

RM18,000 fine.

PP v Mohd Nasaruddin Saron [2017]

Mohd Nasaruddin Saron, 41, a Forex trader was accused of insulting the Prime Minister, Datuk Seri Najib Tun Razak on Facebook on 26 October 2016. The insult was contained in his complaint about the rise in prices of goods and the implementation of goods and services tax (GST).

Charge:

Section 233(1)(a) CMA (pleaded guilty).

Decision of Kuala Lumpur Sessions Court (19/6/2017):

1 day imprisonment and RM4000 fine.

PP v Mohd Shukor Ishak [2017]

Shukor, 30, a factory operator was accused of insulting the Mufti of Perlis Datuk Asri Mohd Zainul Abidin on Facebook on 30 April 2017.

Charge:

Section 233(1)(a) CMA (pleaded guilty).

Decision of Kangar Sessions Court (19/5/2017):

RM2500 fine.

PP v Mohamad Arif Fadila Arbain [2016]

Arif, 26, an unemployed was accused of posting an offensive comment against the Prime Minister Datuk Seri Najib Tun Razak via Twitter using the profile name of @SangAlgojoe on 1 December 2015.

Charge:

Section 233(1)(a) CMA (pleaded guilty).

Decision of Alor Setar Sessions Court (22/11/ 2016):

RM9500 fine.

PP v Rosmin Mohamed Noor [2016]

Rosmin, 40, a postman was accused of insulting the Inspector General of Police Tan Sri Khalid Abu Bakar on Facebook on 22 September 2016.

Charge:

Section 233(1)(a) CMA (pleaded guilty).

Decision of the Cyber Court (11/11/2016):

RM5000 fine or 2 months imprisonment.

PP v Tan Sri Abdul Rahim Thamby Chik [2016]

Tan Sri Abdul Rahim, the former Chief Minister of Melaka was accused of claiming that the Royal Prince of Selangor Tengku Amir Shah became an apostate, on 2015 on Facebook.

Charge:

Section 233(1)(a) CMA (pleaded guilty).

The prosecution decided not to pursue the charge for the same offence under the Sedition Act.

Decision of Shah Alam Sessions Court (20/09/2016):

RM1900 fine or 3 months imprisonment.

The accused paid the fine and apologized to the Royal Prince in a statement in the court read by his lawyer.

| **PP v Muhammad Amirul Azwan Mohd. Shakri [2016]** |
| **Muhammad Amirul Azwan Mohd. Shakri v PP [2016] (HC)** |

Amirul, 19, a labourer was accused of posting offensive comments against the Royal Prince of Johor on TRW Troll Story Facebook page using the profile name of "Miyo Castello" between March to April 2016.

14 comments were posted by "Miyo Castello" to reply to comments posted by the owner of the Facebook page.

Charge:

Section 233(1)(a) CMA (14 charges) (pleaded guilty).

Decision of Kluang Sessions Court (07/06/2016):

1 year imprisonment for each charge.

The prosecution appealed against the decision of the court.

Decision of Kuala Lumpur High Court (15/09/2016):

Quashed the sentence and ordered Amirul to be sent to Henry Gurney School until he reaches the age of 21 years old.

PP v Yunus Hasyim Yaakub [2016]

Yunus, 29, a graphic artist at private company was accused of selling obscene cartoons which he produced himself online at *http://www.gazelleone.net* with a membership fee of RM30 via MOLPoint or Pay Pal.

Charge:

Section 233(2)(a) CMA (pleaded guilty).

Decision of Sepang Sessions Court (19/05/2016):

RM20,000 fine or 5 months imprisonment.

PP v Muhammad Annuar Saberi [2016]

Annuar, 32, a tow truck driver was accused of posting an offensive comment against the Royal Malaysian Police on his Facebook page on 29 December 2015.

Charge:

Section 233(1)(a) CMA.

Decision of Shah Alam Magistrate Court (25/03/2016):

RM5000 fine or 6 months imprisonment.

PP v Muhamad Hafzan Romli [2016]

Hafzan, 26, an electronic factory worker was accused of posting an offensive statement against the Royal Institutions of Johor and Pahang, and the public on Facebook owned by Rashidah Rijal on 6 June 2015. Rashidah, a police officer, was his ex-fiancée.

Rashidah, who was alerted by the post, immediately lodged a police report since she suspected that the posting was done by Hafzan who had her mobile phone's memory card in his possession.

Charge:

Section 233(1)(a) CMA (pleaded guilty).

Decision of Kuala Lumpur Sessions Court (20/01/2016):

RM14,000 fine.

PP v Azmi Yahya [2016]

Azmi was accused of sending an obscene video via email to a lady. The video featured a woman performing oral sex to a man.

Charge:

Section 233(1)(a) CMA (pleaded guilty).

Decision of Kuala Lumpur Sessions Court (15/01/2016):

RM5000 fine.

PP v Adnan Mohd Yunus [2015]

Adnan, 40, a marketing officer at an advertising company was accused of posting an offensive comment against the Sultan of Johor on Astro Awani Facebook page on 17 December 2015.

The comment was posted after the demise of Sultan of Johor's son, Tunku Abdul Jalil.

Charge:

Section 233(1)(a) CMA (pleaded guilty).

Decision of Johor Baharu Magistrate Court (30/12/2015):

RM20,000 fine.

PP v Wan Fatul Johari [2015]

Wan, 68, was accused of was accused of posting an offensive comment against the Sultan of Kelantan on Facebook on 31 August 2012.

He was also accused of posting a statement which insulted the Yang di-Pertuan Agong as the Supreme Head of Malaysia and the Malay Rulers on Facebook on 3 June 2013 and 4 June 2013.

Charge:

Section 233(1)(a) CMA (3 charges).

Decision of Temerloh Sessions Court (30/10/2015):

RM30,000 fine or 8 months imprisonment for the first charge.

RM40,000 fine or 10 months imprisonment for the second charge.

RM50,000 fine or 12 months imprisonment for the third charge.

Wan failed to pay the fine and was ordered to serve imprisonment for 30 months.

PP v Muhammad Hanaffi Rahim [2015]

Hanaffi, 21, a tailor was accused of insulting the late ASP Margaret Tagum Goen, a police officer who used to head an operation which led to the confiscation of his motorcycle. The insult was posted on WeChat within a few hours after the deceased died at the hospital after being hit by some motorcyclists when conducting a road block at Jalan Batu Pahat - Mersing.

Charge:

Section 233(3) CMA (pleaded guilty).

Decision of Batu Pahat Magistrate Court (14/09/2015):

2 months imprisonment and RM2000 fine.

PP v Hoo Wai Men [2015]

Hoo Wai Men, 39, a computer programmer was accused of sending false and obscene content via email and website using the identity of his victim after she rejected his love proposal.

Charge:

Section 233(1)(a) CMA (2 charges) (pleaded guilty).

Decision of Petaling Jaya Sessions Court (03/08/2015):

RM13,000 fine for the first charge.

RM15,000 fine for the second charge.

PP v Rizalman bin Ramli [2015]

Rizalman was accused of posting offensive comments on Facebook.

Charge:

Section 233(1)(a) CMA.

Decision (02/06/2015):

RM2000 fine.

PP v Asnizukacaras bin Saari [2015]

Aznizukacaras, 36, a clerk account was accused of uploading obscene content on "Yamani Salim" blog. He was found in the possession of 67 obscene photos, 35 obscene videos, and a mobile phone containing 2,438 obscene photos and 63 obscene videos.

Charge:

Section 211 CMA (pleaded guilty).

Decision of Kuala Lumpur Sessions Court (28/05/2015):

RM18,000 fine.

Aznizukacaras failed to pay the fine and was ordered to serve imprisonment for 1 month commencing from the date of arrest.

PP v Jasma Aznita [2015]

Jasma was accused of sending offensive content via e-mail.

Charge:

Section 233(1)(a) CMA.

Decision (26/05/2015):

Discharged Jasma with Good Behaviour Bond Order for 3 years under section 294 Criminal Procedure Code.

PP v Huen Chung Sook [2015]

Huen Chung Sook was accused of uploading offensive content at "Casual But Wild Sex" website.

Charge:

Section 233(1)(a) CMA (2 charges).

Decision (26/05/2015):

2 days imprisonment and RM50,000 fine for the 2 charges.

PP v Zulkifli Radzi [2015]

Zulkifli was accused of sending obscene content via MMS.

Charge:

Section 233(1)(a) CMA (3 charges).

Decision (25/05/2015):

RM 3,000 fine.

PP v Mohd Fakhrulradzi Zainal Abidin [2015]

Fakhrulradzi was accused of uploading obscene content on "Jomml" blog.

Charge:

Section 211 CMA (pleaded guilty).

Decision (18/05/2015):

RM 5,000 fine.

PP v Kuan Wai Onn [2015]

Kuan Wai Onn, 49, was accused of selling obscene videos on "rm1069" website for the price of RM20 per piece, with a monthly profit of RM1000.

Charge:
Section 233(2)(a) CMA (pleaded guilty).

Decision of Kuala Lumpur Sessions Court (11/05/2015):
RM30,000 fine.

PP v Amrizal and Muhamad Muhaimin [2015]

Amrizal and Muhaimin were accused of uploading obscene content on "Lucah Teruk" blog.

Charge:
Section 211 CMA (pleaded guilty).

Decision (7/05/2015):
Ordered Compulsory Attendance at the Parole Office: 2 hours a day to 5 working days for 3 months for Amrizal and 2 months for Muhaimin, with a guarantor.

PP v Mohd Azlan bin Ibrahim [2014]

Azlan, 42 was accused of sending obscene SMS and MMS of a photo of a male's private part to his victim, Nor Fadilah on 18 December 2012.

Charge:

Section 233(1)(a) CMA (pleaded guilty).

Decision of Johor Baharu Sessions Court (10/12/2014):

RM3000 fine.

PP v Ahmad Abd Jalil [2013]
Ahmad Abd Jalil v PP [2015] 5 CLJ 480 (HC)

Ahmad was accused of uploading offensive comment against the Sultan of Johor on his Facebook page, using the profile name of "Zul Yahya".

Charges:

Section 233(1)(a) CMA.
Section 233(3) CMA.

Decision of Johor Bahru Sessions Court :

14/04/2013: Discharged Ahmad from the charge under section 233(3) since there was no prima facie case.

21/10/2013: RM20,000 fine for the charge under section 233(1)(a).

Ahmad appealed to the High Court.

Decision of Johor Bahru High Court (27/10/2014):

Dismissed Ahmad's appeal, and retained conviction and sentence.

PP v Effi Nazrel Saharudin [2014]

Effi, 35, a blogger was accused of posting offensive comments which insulted the Yang di-Pertuan Agong on his Twitter account "1Obefiend" on 1 June 2013.

Charge:

Section 233(1)(a) CMA (Changed to guilty plea).

Decision of Kuala Lumpur Sessions Court (15/08/2014):

RM10,000 fine.

PP v. Rutinin Suhaimin [2010]
PP v. Rutinin Suhaimin [2013] 2 CLJ 427 (HC)
PP v. Rutinin Suhaimin [2013]
Rutinin Suhaimin v. PP [2015] 3 CLJ 838 (HC)

Rutinin, 35, a mobile phone retailer was accused of posting comments which insulted the Sultan of Perak on the Guestbook at *http://books.dreambook.com/duli/duli.html* which was linked to the Sultan's Office Website i.e. *http://sultan.perak.gov.my* on 13 February 2009.

The comments were made in response to the Sultan's decision to appoint Datuk Seri Dr. Zambry Abdul Kadir as the new Chief Minister after rejecting the application by the People's Coalition Party to dissolve the State Legislative Assembly.

Charge:
Section 233(1)(a) CMA.

Decision of the Sessions Court (12/07/2010):
Discharged Rutinin since there was no prima facie case.

The prosecution appealed.

Decision of Kota Kinabalu High Court (23/11/2012):

Allowed the appeal by the prosecution and ordered Rutinin to enter his defense at the Sessions Court before another judge since the previous judge was on study leave.

Decision of the Sessions Court (different judge) (21/11/2013):

Fine RM15,000.

Rutinin appealed.

Decision of Kota Kinabalu High Court (18/06/2014):

Allowed Rutinin's appeal, and quashed his conviction.

PP v Samsudin Salleh [2013]

Samsudin was accused of selling obscene materials on "zulshah103" website.

Charge:

Section 233(2)(a) CMA (pleaded guilty).

Decision (01/10/2013):

Ordered Compulsory Attendance at the Parole Office for 4 hours a day for a period of 3 months with a bond of RM2000 and a guarantor.

PP v Ghazali Zainol [2012]

Ghazali was accused of sending obscene SMS.

Charge:

Section 233(1)(a) CMA (pleaded guilty).

Decision (23/10/2012):

RM3000 fine.

Ghazali failed to pay the fine and was ordered to serve imprisonment for 3 months.

PP v Hasdiana Binti Hashim [2012]

Hasdiana was accused of sending obscene SMS.

Charge:

Section 233(1)(a) CMA (pleaded guilty).

Decision (20/10/2012):

RM5000 fine.

Hasdiana failed to pay the fine and was ordered to serve imprisonment for 6 months.

PP v Muslim bin Ahmad [2010]
PP v Muslim bin Ahmad [2010] (HC)
PP v Muslim bin Ahmad [2011]
PP v Muslim bin Ahmad [2013] 1 AMR 436 (HC)

Muslim Ahmad, 54, a businessman was accused of posting comments which insulted the Sultan of Perak on the Guestbook at *http://books.dreambook.com/duli/duli.html* which was linked to the Sultan's Office Website i.e. *http://sultan.perak.gov.my* on 7 and 8 February 2009.

Charge:

Section 233(1)(a) CMA (3 charges).

Decision of Kuala Lumpur Sessions Court (21/06/2010):

Discharged Muslim since there was no prima facie case.

The prosecution appealed.

Decision of Kuala Lumpur High Court (08/12/2010):

Allowed the appeal by the prosecution and ordered Muslim to enter defense at the Sessions Court.

Decision of Kuala Lumpur Sessions Court (07/04/2011):

Discharged Muslim since there was no prima facie case.

The prosecution appealed.

Decision of Kuala Lumpur High Court (28/08/2012):

Allowed the appeal by the prosecution.

RM10,000 fine for each charge.

PP v Khairul Nizam Abd Ghani [2012]

Khairul Nizam, 31, a computer technician was accused of posting insulting statements against the late Sultan of Johor, who used to be the Yang di-Pertuan Agong. The comment was made after the demise of the Sultan on his blog *http://adukataruna.blogspot.com.my* on 22 January 2010.

Charge:

Section 233(1)(a) CMA.

Decision of Seremban Sessions Court (31/05/2012):

Discharged Khairul since there was no prima facie case.

PP v Fatimah Maisurah Abdullah and Anor [2011]

Fatimah, 34, a lawyer and her husband Fuad Ariff Abdul Rashid, 35, a businessman were accused of posting comments which insulted the Sultan of Perak on the Guestbook at *http://books.dreambook.com/duli/duli.html*, linked to the Sultan's Office Website i.e. *http://sultan.perak.gov.my* on 14 February 2009.

Charge:
Section 233(1)(a) CMA.

Decision of Kuala Terengganu Sessions Court (28/07/2011):
Discharged Fatimah and Fuad since there was no prima facie case.

PP v Yazid Mohd Zain [2011]

Yazid was accused of posting offensive comments against the Sultan of Johor.

Charge:
Section 233(1)(a) CMA.

Decision of the Sessions Court:
Discharged Yazid. He later was granted pardon by the Sultan of Johor.

PP v Nor Hisham Osman [2010]
Nor Hisham bin Osman v PP [2010] MLJU 1249

Nor Hisham, 36, a surveyor was accused of posting comments which insulted the Sultan of Perak on the Guestbook at *http://books.dreambook.com/duli/duli.html* which was linked to the Sultan's Office Website i.e. *http://sultan.perak.gov.my* on 11 February 2009.

Charge:

Section 233(1)(a) CMA.

Hisham applied to the Shah Alam High Court to quash the charge on the ground that section 233(1)(a) violates Article 10 of the Federal Constitution which protects freedom of expression, but the High Court dismissed the application on 26 August 2010.

Decision of the Sessions Court:

RM12,000 fine.

Irwan Bin Abdul Rahman [2010]

Irwan, 36, a Malay Mail executive editor who was also a satire blogger using the name Hassan Skodeng was accused of uploading a false article entitled "TNB to sue WWF over Earth Hour" on 25 March 2010.

Charge:

Section 233(1)(a) CMA.

Decision of the Sessions Court:

Discharged Irwan.

Muhammad Noor Bin Ismail [2010]

Muhammad was charged for uploading offensive comments.

Charge:

Section 233(1)(a) CMA (pleaded guilty).

Decision of the Sessions Court:

RM6000 fine.

PP v Maslina Hashim [2010]

Maslina, 32, a resort lobby manager was accused of selling obscene materials on *http://39melayu.com*.

Charge:

Section 233(2)(a) CMA.

Decision of Klang Sessions Court (11/10/2010):

RM5000 fine.

PP v Tajulzairi Tajuddin [2010]

Tajulzairi, 31, a bank clerk was accused of selling obscene materials on *http://www.wanitamelayu2u.com*.

Charge:

Section 233(2)(a) CMA (pleaded guilty).

Decision of Klang Sessions Court (27/05/2010):

RM30,000 fine or 6 months imprisonment.

He was the first person convicted under the provision.

PP v Seah Boon Khim [2009]

Seah, a former employee of EON Bank Bhd was accused of uploading offensive and indecent materials on http://www.xanga.com/hokongchan67 with the intention to annoy Ho Kong Chan, the Head of Audit Department of EON Bank.

Charge:
Section 233(1)(a) CMA (pleaded guilty).

Decision of Kuala Lumpur Sessions Court (7/7/2009):
RM8000 fine.

PP v Azrin bin Md. Zin [2009]

Azrin, 33, a school lab assistant and online trader was accused of posting comments which insulted the Sultan of Perak on the Guestbook at *http://books.dreambook.com/duli/duli.html* which was linked to the Sultan's Office Website i.e. *http://sultan.perak.gov.my* on 12 February 2009.

Charge:
Section 233(1)(a) CMA (pleaded guilty).

Decision of Kuala Lumpur Sessions Court (13/3/2009):
RM10,000 fine. Azrin was the first person charged and convicted under section 233(1)(a) Communication and Multimedia Act.

Offences under the Sedition Act 1948

PP v Wan Ji Wan Hussin [2018]
Wan Ji Wan Hussin v PP [2019]

Wan Ji, 32, a freelance preacher was accused of posting a seditious statement on Facebook using the profile name of "wanji.attaaduddi" against the Sultan of Selangor on 5 November 2012. The statement allegedly questioned the credibility of the Sultan as the Head of Islamic Religion for the state.

Charge:

Section 4(1)(c) Sedition Act.

Wan Ji was allowed by Shah Alam Sessions Court on 16 January 2016 to refer the issue regarding the constitutionality of the Sedition Act to the High Court. It was decided that the Act was not in violation of the Federal Constitution.

Decision of Kuala Lumpur Sessions Court (09/04/2018):

9 months imprisonment.

Wan Ji appealed against the decision. The prosecution also appealed against the sentence

Decision of Shah Alam High Court (09/07/2019):

Dismissed Wan Ji's appeal and allowed the appeal by the prosecution by increasing the sentence to 1 year imprisonment.

Wan Ji has filed an appeal to the Court of Appeal.

PP v S. Arutchelvan [2018]

S. Arutchelvan, a politician was accused of criticising the judiciary on Facebook on 10 February 2015. The statement was made following Datuk Seri Anwar Ibrahim's sodomy conviction.

Charge:

Section 4(1)(b) Sedition Act.

Decision of Kuala Lumpur Sessions Court (15/08/2018):

Discharged and acquitted Arutchelvan after the prosecution withdrew the charge against him.

PP v Eric Paulsen [2018]

Eric, 42, Executive Director of Lawyers for Liberty was accused of posting a seditious statement on Twitter using the profile name of "ericpaulsen101" against the Islamic Development Department of Malaysia. The tweet alleged accused Jakim as promoting extremism every Friday in Malaysia.

Charge:

Section 4(1)(c) Sedition Act.

Decision of Kuala Lumpur Sessions Court (15/08/2018):

Discharged and acquitted Eric after the prosecution withdrew the charge against him.

PP v Zulkiflee Anwar Haque [2018]

Zulkiflee, 53, popularly known as Zunar, was accused of insulting the judiciary in tweets on Twitter made in relation to Datuk Seri Anwar Ibrahim's conviction in the Sodomy 2 case.

Charge:

Section 4(1)(b) Sedition Act (9 charges).

Decision of Kuala Lumpur Sessions Court (30/07/2018):

Discharged and acquitted Zunar after the prosecution withdrew the charges against him.

PP v Mat Shuhaimi bin Shafiei [2011]
Mat Shuhaimi bin Shafiei v Pendakwa Raya [2012] MLJU 93 (HC)
Mat Shuhaimi bin Shafiei v PP [2014] 2 MLJ 145 (COA)
Mat Shuhaimi bin Shafiei v Kerajaan Malaysia [2015] 1 LNS 793 (HC)
Mat Shuhaimi bin Shafiei v Kerajaan Malaysia [2017] 1 CLJ 404 (COA)
Kerajaan Malaysia v Mat Shuhaimi bin Shafiei [2018] 1 LNS 28 (FC)

Mat Shuhaimi, 46, a politician was accused of uploading seditious article regarding the appointment of Selangor State Secretary on his blog *http://srimuda.blogspot.com* on 30 December 2010.

Charge:

Section 4 Sedition Act.

Shuhaimi had filed a notice of motion at Shah Alam High Court seeking for the sedition charge against to be quashed on the ground that the Sedition Act violates Article 10 of the Federal Constitution which protects freedom of expression, but the High Court dismissed the appeal on 26 August 2011.

He further appealed to the Court of Appeal, which also dismissed his appeal on 26 December 2013. He then appealed to the Federal Court, but on 20 October 2014 he withdrew his appeal as he filed a new summons in the Kuala High Court to challenge the constitutionality of the Sedition Act.

However, the High Court dismissed his summons on 22 February 2015. He then appealed to the Court of Appeal.

The Court of Appeal allowed his appeal on 25 November 2016. The court held that Section 3 (3) of the Sedition Act, which states that "intention" does not need to be proved, is unconstitutional.

The government appealed against the decision of the Court of Appeal. The Federal Court on 7 January 2018 allowed the appeal and reinstated the decision of the High Court. The Federal Court ordered the criminal trial in the Sessions Court to proceed.

Shuhaimi died of cancer on 1 July 2018.

PP v Abdullah Zaik Abdul Rahman [2016]

Abdullah Zaik, the President of Ikatan Muslimin Malaysia (Isma), was accused of making a seditious statement in a report entitled "Kedatangan pendatang Cina bersama penjajah British satu bentuk pencerobohan" (The arrival of Chinese immigrants with the British invaders was a form of invasion) published on Isma portal at http://www.ismaweb.net on 6 May 2014.

Charge:

Section 4(1)(c) Sedition Act.

Decision of Petaling Jaya Sessions Court (30/08/2016):

RM2000 fine.

PP v Teresa Kok Suh Sim [2015]
Teresa Kok Suh Sim v PP [2015] AMEJ 1323

Teresa, a politician was accused of posting a seditious video on YouTube, with the title "Teresa Kok ONEderful Malaysia CNY 2014" on 1 February 2014.

Charge:

Section 4(1)(c) Sedition Act.

Teresa applied for the case to be heard by the High Court, but the High Court on 25 June 2015 dismissed her application on the ground that it did not have the merit since the Sessions Court was competent to hear the case.

Decision of Kuala Lumpur Sessions Court (20/11/2015):

Discharged and acquitted Teresa after the prosecution withdrew the charge against her.

PP v Hidayat Mohamed [2015]

Hidayat, 35, a special education teacher at a school in Segambut was accused of posting a seditious Facebook comment which insulted the Hindus during Thaipusam festival. The comment was posted on Facebook page WiFiZoneDesaRejang using the profile name of "Man Nambalast" and "Mohamed Hidayat" on 17 January 2014.

Charge:
Section 4(1)(c) Sedition Act.

Decision of Selayang Sessions Court (18/11/2015):
RM4000 fine.

PP v David Orok [2015]

David, 50, a politician was accused of insulting Islam and Prophet Muhammad on Facebook.

Charge:
Section 4(1)(c) Sedition Act (pleaded guilty).

Decision of Kota Kinabalu High Court (15/09/2015):
16 months imprisonment.

PP v Ali Abd Jalil [2014]

Ali, 29, was accused of insulting the Royal family of Johor and the Sultan Selangor on Facebook.

Charges:

Sedition Act (3 charges).

When he was released on bail on 29 September 2014, Ali absconded to Sweden and sought asylum from the Swedish government.

He was granted asylum in 2014, and permanent residency in 2016.

Offences Affecting the Public Health, Safety, Convenience, Decency and Morals under the Penal Code

PP v A. Visnu Varatan [2019]

Visnu, 29, a technical manager was accused of having in his mobile phone obscene photos and videos on 8 August 2019.

Charge:

Section 292 Penal Code (pleaded guilty).

Decision of Petaling Jaya Magistrate Court (16/08/2019):

RM3,000 fine.

PP v Halim Miah [2019]

Halim, 27, a Bangladeshi was accused of having in his mobile phone obscene videos on 9 February 2019.

Charge:

Section 292 Penal Code (pleaded guilty).

Decision of Ayer Keroh Magistrate Court (22/03/2019):

1 year imprisonment.

PP v FC Dailova [2018]

Dailova, 24, a restaurant worker of Myanmar nationality was accused of having in his mobile phone obscene photos on 23 September 2018.

Charge:

Section 292 Penal Code (pleaded guilty).

Decision of Petaling Jaya Magistrate Court (11/10/2018):

4 months imprisonment.

PP v K.K. Ravi [2018]

Ravi, 33, a factory worker was accused of having possession in his mobile phone obscene photos and videos in September 2016.

Charge:

Section 292 Penal Code (pleaded guilty).

Decision of Ipoh Magistrate Court (30/03/2018):

RM7000 fine.

PP v Mohd Ismail Muda [2017]

Ismail, 36, a cleaner was accused of sending an obscene photo via WhatsApp to his 19 year old neighbour on 18 September 2016.

Charge:

Section 292 Penal Code (pleaded guilty).

Decision of Kota Bharu Magistrate Court (26/09/2017):

RM3000 fine.

PP v Khoo Teng Chong [2017]

Khoo, 32, an IT executive was accused of having possession in his mobile phone 2 obscene oriented video clips at Pavilion Kuala Lumpur on 9 August 2017.

The clips were his filming of under the skirts of women taking the escalator in the building.

Charge:

Section 292 Penal Code (pleaded guilty).

Decision of Kuala Lumpur Magistrate Court (11/08/2017):

RM2500 fine.

PP v Kenneth Chong Po-Ken [2017]

Kenneth, 33, an insurance consultant was accused of having possession in his Western Digital disc obscene photos of his ex girlfriend on 30 May 2017.

Charge:
Section 292 Penal Code (pleaded guilty).

Decision of Kuala Lumpur Magistrate Court (07/06/2017):
RM3000 fine.

PP v Bashir Khan Abib Rahman [2017]

Bashir, 32, a hospital security guard was accused of having possession in his mobile phone an obscene video of himself and a teenager on 2 March 2017. The video was recorded by him on 13 February 2017 when he and the 17 year old teenager (whom he virtually met the previous day via WeChat) were having sex in a hotel room.

Charge:
Section 292 Penal Code (pleaded guilty).

Decision of Ampang Magistrate Court (09/03/2017):
RM10,000 fine.

PP v Taslinnaim Tasrip [2017]

Taslinnaim, 24, a restaurant waiter was accused of having possession in his mobile phone some obscene photos and video at a shopping mall in Jalan Tun Sambanthan on 5 January 2017.

He was earlier arrested when the police received a report that he was involved in a rape case and had seized his mobile phone.

He was also found distributing the videos and pictures via WhatsApp to a 19-year-old college student who was allegedly the rape victim.

Charge:

Section 292 Penal Code (pleaded guilty).

Decision of Kuala Lumpur Sessions Court (13/02/2017):

12 months imprisonment.

He was also accused of rape under Section 376 Penal Code, but he pleaded not guilty.

| **PP v Bam Bahadur Bhetal [2017]** |

Bahadur, 29, a cleaner from Nepal was accused of having possession in his mobile phone 5 obscene photos.

Charge:

Section 292 Penal Code (pleaded guilty).

Decision of Johor Bahru Magistrate Court (06/02/2017):

12 months imprisonment.

| **PP v Sulaiman Valiyapeedika Mundakkundil [2017]** |

Sulaiman, 36, an Indian citizen working as a shop assistant was accused of having possession in his mobile phone more than 100 obscene drawings, photos and videos of children on 3 January 2017.

Charge:

Section 292 Penal Code (pleaded guilty).

Decision of Kota Tinggi Magistrate Court (16/01/2017):

12 months imprisonment.

PP v Mohd Azam Manap @ Awang [2012]

Azam, 32, a lorry driver was accused of having possession in his mobile phone 13 obscene videos on 31 July 2008.

Charge:
Section 292 Penal Code (pleaded guilty).

Decision of Kuala Terengganu Magistrate Court (11/07/2012):
RM1500 fine.

PP v Datuk Shazryl Eskay Abdullah and Ors [2011]

Datuk Shazryl Eskay Abdullah, Datuk Shuib Lazim and Tan Sri Rahim Thamby Chik were accused of screening an obscene video of a woman and a guy at Seri Makmur Room, Carcosa Seri Negara Hotel, Kuala Lumpur to a group of journalists on 21 March 2011. They claimed that the guy in the video was Datuk Seri Anwar Ibrahim, their political opponent.

Charge:
Section 292(a) Penal Code read with Section 34 (pleaded guilty).

Decision of Kuala Lumpur Magistrate Court :
RM3000 fine (Eskay).

RM1500 fine (Shuib).

RM1000 fine (Rahim).

Offences Relating to Criminal Intimidation, Insult and Annoyance under the Penal Code

PP v Mohamad Nadzreekusairi Shariff [2019]

Nadzreekusairi, 37, a tailor was accused of insulting his friend's daughter by uploading the girl's photo on Intagram with an offensive caption between 29 and 30 April 2019. The photo was deleted after the victim contacted him but the still kept them in his IG story.

Charge:

Section 509 Penal Code (pleaded guilty).

Decision of Ampang Magistrate Court (30/05/2019):

RM3500 fine.

PP v Mohd Zamri Mohd Yunus [2019]

Zamri, 37, a food delivery guy was accused of sending a murder threat message via WhatsApp to his ex-wife Marina Ibrahim on 4 February 2019.

Charge:

Section 507 Penal Code (pleaded guilty).

Decision of Kuala Lumpur Magistrate Court (08/02/2019):

RM3000 fine.

PP v Muhamat Mustazah Mukhtar [2019]

Mustazah, 34, an unemployed was accused of sending an obscene message via WhatsApp to a lady on 17 December 2018.

Charge:

Section 509 Penal Code (pleaded guilty).

Decision of Kuala Lumpur Magistrate Court (29/01/2019):

5 months imprisonment.

PP v Muhammad Omar Aliff Rosli [2018]

Omar, 32, a mechanic was accused of editing his ex-girlfriend photos by making them appear obscene and sending the photos via WhatsApp to her between January and August 2017.

Charge:

Section 509 Penal Code (pleaded guilty).

Decision of Kuala Lumpur Magistrate Court (07/09/2018):

RM5000 fine.

PP v Abdul Hafiz Rahim [2018]

Hafiz, 28, a masseur was accused of sending murder threat messages via WhatsApp to his employer Fakhita Halim and her husband Muhamad Shafie Zulkarai on 14 November 2017.

Charge:

Section 507 Penal Code (2 charges)(pleaded guilty).

Decision of Kuala Lumpur Magistrate Court (18/01/2018):

RM6000 fine.

PP v Chow Chee Yeep [2017]

Chow, 31, a cook was accused of taking pictures and making a video recording, using his mobile phone, of a female sales promoter's leg at a food court in Pavilion Shopping Mall on 13 June 2016.

Charge:

Section 509 Penal Code (pleaded guilty).

Decision of Kuala Lumpur Magistrate Court (25/07/2017):

RM1000 fine.

PP v Mohamad Rizki Hamidasli [2017]

Rizki, 35, a salesperson was accused of sending an obscene photo of his private part to a 14 years old girl via WeChat on 8 July 2017. He also asked for the nude photo of the victim and her private part, and persuaded the victim to have sex at a hotel.

Charge:

Section 509 Penal Code (pleaded guilty).

Decision of Kuala Lumpur Magistrate Court (18/07/2017):

RM2500 fine.

PP v Muhammad Nasrul Wafiy Harizan [2017]

Nasrul, 25, a trader was accused of sending an obscene photo via WhatsApp to a police officer on 28 March 2017. He introduced himself as the cousin of an individual who was being investigated by her for the offence of domestic violence, and threatened to disseminate her phone number.

Charge:

Section 509 Penal Code (pleaded guilty).

Decision of Kuala Lumpur Magistrate Court (03/04/2017):

RM4000 fine.

PP v Alsaik [2017]

Alsaik, 28, a shop assistant was accused of taking pictures, using his mobile phone, of two sisters in a changing room in Sunway Velocity, Cheras on 12 March 2017.

Charge:

Section 509 Penal Code (pleaded guilty).

Decision of Kuala Lumpur Magistrate Court (15/03/2017):

RM3000 fine.

PP v Abdul Rahim Mohd Abas [2017]

Rahim, 34, an unemployed was accused of sending a photo of his private part and obscene message to a woman via mobile phone on 7 January 2017.

Charge:

Section 509 Penal Code (pleaded guilty).

Decision of Kuala Lumpur Magistrate Court (13/01/2017):

1 month imprisonment.
RM1500 fine.

PP v Cher Phoh Shien [2016]

Cher, 25, was accused of filming, using his mobile phone, a lady in a changing room in Dataran Pahlawan Melaka Megamall on 16 October 2016.

Charge:

Section 509 Penal Code (pleaded guilty).

Decision of Ayer Keroh Magistrate Court (19/10/2016):

3 days imprisonment.

RM2500 fine.

PP v David Ng Qi Long [2016]

David, 22, a salesperson was accused of screening an obscene video via his mobile phone to two of his neighbour's sons who were underaged on 8 September 2016.

Charge:

Section 509 Penal Code (pleaded guilty).

Decision of Kuala Lumpur Magistrate Court (13/09/2016):

RM2500 fine.

PP v Long Jhow Weh [2015]

Long, 27, a real property agent was accused of filming, using his mobile phone, under the skirt of a lady taking the escalator in Midvalley Mega Mall on 8 August 2015. His mobile phone also contained other similar videos.

Charge:

Section 509 Penal Code (pleaded guilty).

Decision of Kuala Lumpur Magistrate Court (11/08/2015):

10 days imprisonment.

RM6000 fine.

PP v Nasrul Aizat Zulkifli [2015]

Nasrul, 25, an engineer was accused of filming, using his mobile phone, under the skirt of a lady taking the escalator in Low Yat Plaza, on 13 June 2015.

Charge:

Section 509 Penal Code (pleaded guilty).

Decision of Kuala Lumpur Magistrate Court (16/06/2015):

5 days imprisonment.

RM4000 fine.

PP v Jamilah Othman [2014]

Jamilah, 30, was accused of sending a threatening message via SMS to her husband, Shahrir Firdaus Nor Ramlai on 11 June 2014.

Charge:

Section 507 Penal Code (pleaded guilty).

Decision of Ayer Keroh Magistrate Court (08/07/2014):

RM2500 fine.

PP v Lum Gah Wai [2014]

Lum, 27, was accused of threatening to electronically disseminate his ex-girlfriend's nude photographs which were stored in his two mobile phones after she refused to assist him in paying his debt to a loan shark on 23 April 2013.

Charge:

Section 509 Penal Code (pleaded guilty).

Decision of Sibu Magistrate Court (05/05/2014):

RM3000 fine.

Lum opted for the 3 months imprisonment in default since he could not afford to pay the fine.

PP v Mohd Roslan Ahmad [2012]

Roslan, 46, a dispatch rider was accused of threatening Joanne Low, a consular officer of the British High Commission by leaving a message via his mobile phone to her voicemail box by saying, "watch out for terrorist attack" on 19 August 2012.

Charge:

Section 507 Penal Code (pleaded guilty).

Decision of Kuala Lumpur Magistrate Court (02/11/2012):

RM3000 fine.

PP v Mohd Ruslaini Rais [2012]

Ruslaini, 49, was accused of sending obscene SMS to a professional masseuse (who was also a single mother) after using the victim's service on 28 December 2011.

Charge:

Section 509 Penal Code.

Decision of Kuala Terengganu Magistrate Court (03/05/2012):

3 months imprisonment.

Offences Relating to Extortion and Defamation under the Penal Code

---

PP v Rafizi Ramli [2019]

Rafizi, a politician was accused of defaming Tabung Haji by posting on his Facebook page an article with the title "Analisa Kewangan Tabung Haji 2009-2015" on 9 February 2016.

Charge:

Section 499 Penal Code.

Decision of Kuala Lumpur Magistrate Court (27/02/2019):

Discharged and acquitted Rafizi after the prosecution withdrew the charge against him.

PP v Muhammad Faez Aiman Toiban [2017]

Faez, 23, a security guard was accused of sending a threatening message via WhatsApp to a lady that he would disseminate her nude photo if she did not pay him RM5000 on 7 February 2017.

Charge:

Section 385 Penal Code (pleaded guilty).

Decision of Kuala Lumpur Magistrate Court (23/02/2017):

RM3500 fine.

PP v Muhammad Shazarul Ikhmal Rospisham [2016]

Shazarul, 20, an unemployed was accused of sending 20 nude photos of his ex-girlfriend via WeChat to her on 10 January 2016 and threatening to post them online if she failed to pay him RM200 for each of the photo.

Charge:

Section 384 Penal Code.

Decision of Kuala Lumpur Magistrate Court (12/02/2016):

RM4000 fine.

PP v Rahimah Salin [2015]

Rahimah, a traffic offender was accused of insulting and defaming a Magistrate on her Facebook page "Iema.elyzam". She posted that the sentence of RM1300 fine against her by the Magistrate for the traffic offence was inconsiderate since she was a single mother.

Charge:

Section 499 Penal Code (pleaded guilty).

Decision of Ayer Keroh Magistrate Court (07/07/2015):

7 days imprisonment and RM1500 fine.

PP v Dato' Dr Ahmad Ramzi Bin Ahmad Zubir [2011]
Dato' Dr Ahmad Ramzi Bin Ahmad Zubir v PP [2013]
PP v Dato' Dr Ahmad Ramzi Bin Ahmad Zubir [2015] 6 CLJ 1028 (COA)

Ramzi, 43, the former political secretary of Terengganu Chief Minister was accused of sending SMS to threaten 3 former People's Representatives from the National Front party and defamatory SMS defamation to the former Senior Confidential Secretary (SUSK) of the Chief Minister on 2009.

Charges:

Section 500 and 507 Penal Code (4 charges).

Decision of Kuala Terengganu Sessions Court (28/11/2011):

3 months imprisonment for each charge.

The sentences were ordered to run consecutively.

Ramzi appealed to the High Court.

Decision of Kuala Terengganu High Court (29/12/2013):

Allowed Ramzi's appeal against conviction.

The prosecution appealed to the Court of Appeal.

Decision of the Court of Appeal (25/11/2014):

Allowed the appeal by the prosecution.

Retained the earlier sentence by the Sessions Court, but ordered the sentence to run concurrently.

Offences Relating to Terrorism under the Penal Code

PP v Ahmad Azmi Ahmad Rosli & Mahadi Ibrahim [2018]
Ahmad Azmi Ahmad Rosli v PP [2019] 1 LNS 358
Mahadi Ibrahim v PP [2019]

Azmi, 25, and Mahadi, 34, both working as labourers, were accused of receiving a training instruction via WhatsApp group "The Rise of Jundullah" in making explosives from Muhamad Hafizi, a person ready to engage in a terrorist activity on 23 September 2017. They were also accused of being present at the training place in Pasir Puteh, Kelantan on 10 October 2017, knowing that the training was for the preparation to engage in a terror attack against the Better Festival Beer 2017 in Kuala Lumpur.

Azmi was also accused of having possession in his mobile phone 20 photos, 3 videos and 16 documents related to Daesh on 10 October 2017.

Charges:

Section 130FA(a) Penal Code.

Section 130FB(1)(a) Penal Code.

Section 130JB(1)(a) Penal Code (against Azmi only).

Decision of Kuala Lumpur High Court (20/04/2018):

14 years imprisonment for the first charge.

5 years imprisonment for the second charge.

3 years imprisonment (third charge) (against Azmi only).

Azmi and Mahadi separately appealed against the sentences.

Decision of the Court of Appeal upon Azmi's appeal (01/04/2019):

Dismissed the appeal.

Decision of the Court of Appeal upon Mahadi's appeal (08/07/2019):

Dismissed the appeal.

PP v Nor Mizan Panijan [2019]

Mizan, 40, a cab driver was accused of showing support to Daesh in Telegram group "Gagak Hitam" on 30 March 2016 to 12 April 2016.

He was also accused of managing a terrorist's property by depositing RM70 to a Maybank account owned by Mohd Haniffa Syedul Akbar on 1 February 2016, and depositing RM20 to a Maybank account owned by Bukhori Che Noor on 4 April 2016 for the purpose of terrorism.

He was also accused of having possession in his mobile phone 21 videos and 10 photos related to Daesh.

Charges:

Section 130J(1)(a) Penal Code.

Section 130Q(1) Penal Code.

Section 130JB(1)(a) Penal Code.

Decision of Kuala Lumpur High Court (28/05/2019):

10 years imprisonment for the first charge.

6 years imprisonment for the second charge.

3 years imprisonment for the third charge.

PP v Aszroy bin Achoi [2018] 9 MLJ 702
PP v Aszroy bin Achoi [2019]

Aszroy, 25, was accused of supporting Daesh via his two Facebook accounts "Yohyo Irranun Peace AlBorneozy" and "Yohyo Illa'nun AlSaba Malizia" between 8 May to 19 July 2016. He was also accused of having possession in his mobile phone 43 images associated with Daesh.

Charges:

Section 130J(1)(a) Penal Code.

Section 130JB(1)(a) Penal Code.

Decision of Kota Kinabalu High Court (28/10/2017):

7 years imprisonment for the first charge.

2 years imprisonment for the second charge.

The sentences were ordered to run consecutively from the date of arrest.

The prosecution appealed against sentence.

Decision of the Court of Appeal (18/03/2019):

Dismissed the appeal.

PP v Mohamad Nasuha bin Abdul Razak [2017] MLJU 1476
Mohamad Nasuha bin Abdul Razak v PP [2019]

Nasuha, 40, a rubber dealer, was accused of showing support to Daesh in Telegram group "Gagak Hitam" on 30 March 2016. He was also accused of having possession in his mobile phone 4 photos related to Daesh.

He was also accused of transferring a total amount of RM 200 via Maybank to a person to support terrorist activities on 4 May and 29 June 2016.

Charges:

Section 130JB(1)(a) Penal Code.

Section 130JB(1)(a) Penal Code.

Section 130N(b) (2 charges).

Decision of Kuala Lumpur High Court (06/09/2017):

13 years imprisonment for the first charge.

4 years imprisonment for the second charge.

10 years imprisonment for the third charge.

10 years imprisonment for the fourth charge.

Nasuha appealed against the sentence.

Decision of the Court of Appeal (15/01/2019):

Allowed the appeal and set aside the sentence of 13 years imprisonment and substituted it with 10 years imprisonment from the date of arrest.

Affirmed the sentences imposed by the High Court in respect of the second, third and fourth charges.

PP v Razis Awang [2018]

Razis, 32, a secondary school teacher was accused of showing support to Daesh in Telegram group "Gagak Hitam" on 30 March 2016.

He was also accused of having possession in his mobile phone 6 photos and on his laptop 3 photos related to Daesh on 28 September 2017.

Charges:

Section 130J(1)(a) Penal Code.
Section 130JB(1)(a) Penal Code.

Decision of Kuala Lumpur High Court (17/12/2018):

7 years imprisonment for the first charge.
2 years imprisonment for the second charge.

PP v Wan Mohamad Nur Firdaus bin Abd Wahab [2017] MLJU 1793
PP v Wan Mohamad Nur Firdaus bin Abd Wahab & Another Appeal [2019] 5 CLJ 320

Firdaus, 22, an unemployed, was accused of showing support to Daesh in Telegram group "Gagak Hitam" from 25 March 2016 until 25 September 2016. He was also accused of having possession in his mobile phone 23 photos related to Daesh.

Charges:

Section 130J(1)(a) Penal Code.

Section 130JB(1)(a) Penal Code.

Decision of Kuala Lumpur High Court (06/09/2017):

8 years imprisonment for the first charge.

5 years imprisonment for the second charge.

Firdaus and the Public Prosecutor both appealed against the sentences.

Decision of the Court of Appeal (18/09/2018):

Dismissed the Public Prosecutor's appeal.

Allowed Firdaus's appeal by reducing the sentence of the first charge to 5 years' imprisonment and that of the second charge to 2 years imprisonment.

PP v Mohd Shahrullizam Ramli [2017]
Mohd Shahrullizam Ramli v PP [2018]

Shahrullizam, 31, a zookeper was accused of showing support to Daesh through Telegram using the profile name of "Sharul" bertween 25 March to 29 June 2016.

His Telegram posts were uploaded before and after the bombing incident at Movida night club between 25 March to 29 June 2016.

He was also accused of having in his possession items related to Daesh including a car sticker, flag and headband bearing Daesh logo.

Charges:

Section 130J(1)(a) Penal Code.

Section 130JB(1)(a) Penal Code.

(pleaded guilty to all charges).

Decision of Kuala Lumpur High Court (15/08/2017):

10 years imprisonment.

3 years imprisonment.

He appealed against sentence:

Decision of the Court of Appeal (24/08/2018):

Dismissed the appeal.

PP v Mohd Fairul Azhar Jaafar [2018]

Fairul, 34, a factory quality controller was accused of having in his pendrive documents, audios and videos related to Daeshon 25 May 2017. The materials were auto downloaded to his mobile phone through the Telegram apps "Risalah Mujahid" before he transferred them to his pendrive.

Charge:

Section 130JB(1) (a) Penal Code.

(pleaded guilty).

Decision of Kuala Lumpur High Court (24/07/2018):

3 years imprisonment.

PP v Muhamad Hafizi Mat Jusoh [2018]

Hafizi, 20, was accused of delivering a training instruction via WhatsApp group "The Rise of Jundullah" in making explosives for a terrorist activity on 23 September 2017. He was also accused of being present at the training place in Pasir Puteh, Kelantan on 10 October 2017 for the preparation to engage in a terror attack against the Better Festival Beer 2017 in Kuala Lumpur.

Hafizi was also accused of having possession in his mobile phone 57 materials related to Daesh and 2 materials related to Al-Qaeda, and posting 13 videos and 5 photos related to Daesh, Al-Qaeda and Jemaah Ansharut Tauhid to his Instagram account under the profile "al_akh_fillah". on 10 October 2017.

Charges:

Section 130FA(a) Penal Code.

Section 130FB(1)(a) Penal Code.

Section 130JB(1)(a) Penal Code.

Section 130JB(1)(b) Penal Code.

Decision of Kuala Lumpur High Court (21/05/2018):

9 years imprisonment for the first charge.

5 years imprisonment for the second charge.

3 years imprisonment for the third charge.

3 years imprisonment for the fourth charge.

PP v Muhamad Noor Helmy Mohd Sabri [2017]
Muhamad Noor Helmy Mohd Sabri v PP [2018]

Helmy, 31, a canteen assistant was accused of having in his possession a t-shirt bearing Daesh logo on 17 March 2017 and showing support giving support to Daesh via the Telegram messaging service, using the profile "Abu Suffyan".

Charges:

Section 130JB(1)(a) Penal Code.

Section 130J (1)(a) Penal Code.

(pleaded guilty to all charges).

Decision of Kuala Lumpur High Court (25/07/2017):

3 years imprisonment for the first charge.

10 years imprisonment for the second charge.

Helmy appealed against the sentences.

Decision of the Court of Appeal (04/04/2018):

Dismissed the appeal.

PP v Jailani Jurimi [2018]

Jailani, 41 a retailer was accused of having possession in his mobile phone 15 copies of Dabiq magazine, 10 copies of Rumiyah magazine and 2 copies of Waislama magazine on 7 August 2017. All the magazines are related to Daesh.

Charge:

Section 130JB(1)(a) Penal Code (pleaded guilty).

Decision of Kuala Lumpur High Court (22/03/2018):

4 years imprisonment.

PP v Tonny Indra Prayitna [2018]

Tonny, a night marker seller, was accused of having possession in his mobile phone 34 photos related to Daesh in 2017.

Charges:

Section 130JB(1)(a) Penal Code (pleaded guilty).

Decision of Kuala Lumpur High Court (01/03/2018):

3 years and 6 months imprisonment.

PP v Zefrul Hashim (2018)

Zefrul, 40, a farmer was accused of showing support to Daesh and Abu Sayyaf by encouraging one "Zahra Alisha" via Facebook Messenger apps to leave Malaysia to join terrorists in Philippines. The offence was committed using the profile name of "Abu Qaqa" between 18 February and 9 March 2017.

He was also accused of having possession in his mobile phone 109 photos and 116 videos related to Daesh on 6 March 2017.

Charges:

Section 130J(1)(a) Penal Code.

Section 130JB(1)(a) Penal Code.

Decision of Kuala Lumpur High Court (17/01/2018):

8 years imprisonment for the first charge.

3 years imprisonment for the second charge.

PP v Mustaza Abdul Rahman [2018] 9 CLJ 101

Mustaza, 30, a police officer was accused of showing support to usage of explosive in terrorist activities via Telegram group "Amanah(phb) v. Pas". He was also accused of hiding the information about terrorists on 30 March 2016 until 29 June 2016 when he had the reason to believe that some offences had been committed.

He was also accused of showing support to Daesh in Telegram group "Gagak Hitam" on 30 March 2016.

Charges:

Section 130J(1)(b) Penal Code.

Section 130M Penal Code.

Section 130J(1)(a) Penal Code.

Decision of Kuala Lumpur High Court (18/12/2017):

12 years imprisonment for the first charge.

7 years imprisonment for the second charge.

12 years imprisonment for the third charge.

PP v Irma Julyanti Buang [2017]

Irma, 32, an assistant engineer was accused of showing support to Daesh via Google+ apps from January 2016 to 20 April 2017.

Charge:

Section 130J(1)(a) Penal Code.

Decision of Kuala Lumpur High Court (29/12/2017):

8 years imprisonment.

PP v Rosmizam Che Din [2017]

Rosmizam Che Din v PP [2017]

Rosmizam, 28, an assistant cook was accused of showing support to Daesh in Telegram group "Gagak Hitam" using the profile name of "Zam Rosden Di", and having possession in his mobile phone 34 photos and 2 videos related to Daesh in 2016.

Charges:

Section 130J(1)(a) Penal Code and

Section 130JB(1)(a) Penal Code (pleaded guilty to all charges).

Decision of Kuala Lumpur High Court (12/07/2017):

6 years imprisonment for the first charge.

2 years imprisonment for the second charge.

Rosmizam appealed against sentence.

Decision of the Court of Appeal (11/12/2017):

Dismissed the appeal.

PP v Rino Kaswara Kasmar [2017]

Rino, 32, an Indonesian tailor was accused of showing support to Daesh in Telegram group "AnsharulKhilaafah Filibiin Indonesia-Filipina" using the profile name of "Rijal Mujahideen Minangkabau" on 2 May 2016.

He was also accused of encouraging others to join Mujahideen Indonesia Timur (MIT) terrorist group and Daesh in the same Telegram group between 2 May to 12 June 2016, and having possession in his mobile phone 83 photos related to Daesh on 12 June 2016.

Charges:

Section 130J(1)(a) Penal Code.

Section 120G(b) Penal Code.

Section 130JB(1)(a) Penal Code.

(pleaded guilty).

Decision of Kuala Lumpur High Court (21/11/2017):

8 years imprisonment for the first charge.

8 years imprisonment for the second charge.

3 years imprisonment for the third charge.

PP v Muhammad Safuan Mohd [2017]

Safuan, 29, a technician was accused of showing support to Daesh in Telegram group "Gagak Hitam" using the profile name of "Abu Marwan Salaki" on 30 May 2016.

He was also accused of having possession in his mobile phone 72 videos, 19 photos ad 419 documents related to Daesh on 6 October 2016.

Charges:

Section 130J(1)(a) Penal Code.

Section 130JB(1)(a) Penal Code (pleaded guilty).

Decision of Kuala Lumpur High Court (19/10/2017):

8 years imprisonment for the first charge.

3 years imprisonment for the second charge.

PP v Tengku Shukri Che Engku Hashim [2017] 1 LNS 1763

Shukri, 31, a businessman was accused of was accused of showing support to Daesh in Telegram group "Gagak Hitam" on 30 March 2016.

He was also charged with giving support to terrorist acts in the use of explosives with the intention to further Daesh ideology through the Telegram app of the "amanah (phb) vs pas" group on 28 June 2016.

Charges:

Section 130J(1)(a) Penal Code.

Section 130J(1)(b) Penal Code.

Decision of Kuala Lumpur High Court (01/08/2017):

8 years imprisonment for the first charge.

3 years imprisonment for the second charge.

PP v Hizmi Razli Abdul Rahim [2017]

Hizmi, 33, an online foreign exchange trader was accused of showing support to Daesh in Telegram group "Gagak Hitam" using the profile name of "Abu Al-Farish" in 2016.

Charge:

Section 130J(1)(a) Penal Code (pleaded guilty).

Decision of Kuala Lumpur High Court (17/07/2017):

8 years imprisonment.

PP v Muhammad Hakimin Azman [2017] MLJU 1024

Hakimin, 31, a computer technician was accused of having in his possession 7 photos related to Daesh on 25 September 2016. The photos, which were found on his Dropbox application in his laptop, looked like ordinary photos of him and his wife in bridal dresses but on the top right of each photo was a small writing of "la illa haillallah" in Arabic and a small Daesh logo.

Charge:

Section 130JB(1)(a) Penal Code (pleaded guilty).

Decision of Kuala Lumpur High Court (20/06/2017):

1 year imprisonment.

PP v Azizi Abdullah [2017] MLJU 649

Azizi, 21, a restaurant worker was accused of showing support to terrorists using explosives, in Telegram groups "Gagak Hitam" and "Amanah vs PAS". He was also a member of the 2 groups which supported the activities of Daesh.

His Telegram posts were uploaded before and after the bombing incident at Movida night club in Puchong between 25 March to 29 June 2016.

He was also accused of having in his possession 1 flag, videos and books about Daesh. His mobile phone also contained photos of Daesh holding firearms.

Charges:

Section 130JB(1)(b) Penal Code.

Section 130JB(1)(a) Penal Code (2 charges).

(pleaded guilty to all charges).

Decision of Kuala Lumpur High Court (25/04/2017):

13 years imprisonment for the first charge.

4 years imprisonment for the second charge.

4 years imprisonment for the third charge.

The sentences were ordered to run consecutively.

PP v Imam Wahyudin bin Karjono & Jonius Ondie @ Jahali
[2017] 1 LNS 691

Imam, 20, an unemployed and Jonius, 24, a factory worker were accused of hurling a grenade at the Movida club which injured eight people. They were also accused of showing support to Daesh in Telegram group "Gagak Hitam" in 2016.

Charges:

Section 130C(1)(b) Penal Code.

Section 130J(1)(a) Penal Code.

(pleaded guilty to all charges).

Decision of Kuala Lumpur High Court (29/03/2017):

25 years imprisonment for the first charge.

10 years imprisonment for the second charge.

PP v Roshelmyzan bin Husain [2017]

Roshelmyzan, 33, a boiler maintenance personnel was accused of showing support to Daesh in Telegram group "Gagak Hitam" in 2016. He was also accused of having possession in his mobile phone a video and an image related to Daesh.

Charges:

Section 130J(1)(a) Penal Code.

Section 130JB(1)(a) Penal Code.

(pleaded guilty to all charges)

Decision of Kuala Lumpur High Court (28/02/2017):

4 years imprisonment for the first charge.

2 years imprisonment for the second charge.

PP v Zairosfitri Jainuddin Azhar [2017]

Zairosfitri, 24, a farmer was accused of showing support to Daesh in Telegram group "Gagak Hitam" on 25 March 2016 to 17 June 2016.

Charge:

Section 130J(1)(a) Penal Code. (pleaded guilty)

Decision of Kuala Lumpur High Court (07/02/2017):

5 years imprisonment.

PP v Mohd Haniffa Syedul Abbar [2016] MLJU 1270

Haniffa, 36, a money changer was accused of indirectly managing a terrorist's property by allowing the transfer of RM19,260 into his Maybank account from his friend Muhammad Wanndy bin Mohamed Jedi who was a Daesh member in Syria after communicating with him via WeChat.

Haniffa had further transferred RM14,800 from the amount to other 11 accounts as directed by Wanndy. The transactions were done between 26 January 2016 to 22 March 2016. Wanndy was a major pioneer in recruiting Malaysians to join Daesh.

Haniffa was also accused of having 17 photos about Daesh and 13 volumes of "Dabiq" magazine in PDF formats, which were also about Daesh, in his mobile phone.

Charges:
Section 130Q(1) and 130JB(1)(a) Penal Code (pleaded guilty).

Decision of Kuala Lumpur High Court (29/09/2016):
10 years imprisonment for the first charge commencing from the date of arrest: 22/3/2016.
2 years imprisonment for the second charge after completing the imprisonment term for the first charge.

PP v Muhammad Sani Mahdi Sahar [2016] MLJU 1106

Sani, 23, a canteen supervisor, was accused of having possession in his mobile phone 39 video clips about Daesh on 9 November 2015, downloaded from websites like isdarat.tv, isdarat.xyz and heavy.com. He was also found to have shown the clips to his friends.

Charge:

Section 130JB(1)(a) Penal Code (pleaded guilty).

Decision of Kuala Lumpur High Court (28/09/2016):

18 months imprisonment.

PP v Anuar Ab Rawi [2016] MLJU 533

Anuar, 40, a freelance preacher was accused of having possession in his mobile phone 4 photos which showed support to Daesh on 22 March 2016. One photo showed terrorists holding a beheaded head. He was also accused of having in his possession a book entitled "Misteri Pasukan Panji Hitam" (the Mystery of the Black Flag Group) about Jemaah Islamiah and Al-Qaeda.

Charge:

Section 130JB(1)(a) Penal Code (pleaded guilty).

Decision of Kuala Lumpur High Court (11/08/2016):

2 years imprisonment.

PP v Azlee Md Salleh [2015]

Azlee, 30, a decor businessman was accused of having possession in his mobile phone a photo of Daesh flag on 19 August 2015.

Azlee was discovered to have started communicating with Malaysians who joined Daesh in Syria including Zulqarnain Ghaz, an ex freelance preacher who was shot during war in Syria. Zulqarnain informed Azlee that police was looking for him, and he sought financial assistance from Azlee.

Zulqarnain was sentenced to 9 years imprisonment by Kuala Lumpur High Court on 9 October 2016 after he pleaded guilty to the charge of entering Syria to support terrorists.

Charge:
Section 130JB(1)(a) Penal Code.

Decision of Kuala Lumpur High Court (03/11/2015):
9 months imprisonment.

PP v Azizah Md Yusof [2015]

Azizah, 54, a housewife was accused of showing support to Daesh via Facebook using the profile name of 'Wan Jah" and "Azizah Yusof" in 2014.

Charges:

Section 130J(1)(b) Penal Code (2 charges) (pleaded guilty).

Decision of Kuala Lumpur High Court (23/10/2015):

2 years and 6 months imprisonment for the first charge.

2 years and 6 months imprisonment for the second charge.

PP v Nazirul Abidin Thalha [2015]

Nazirul, 24, a jobless guy was accused of having 15 publications, on terrorists and terrorism activities, which were downloaded to his mobile phone on 2 July 2015. Among the publications were Miracles in Syria, Black Flags From Syria Revolution and How To Survive In The West 2015: A Mujahid Guide.

Charge:

Section 130JB(1)(a) Penal Code.

Decision of Kuala Lumpur High Court (11/9/2015):

12 months imprisonment.

Nazirul became the first person charged and sentenced to imprisonment under Section 130JB(1)(a) which came into operation on 15 Jun 2015. He was also the 5th individual who was imprisoned for offences related to terrorism.

Mutiple Offences under the Penal Code, Communication and Multimedia Act, Sedition Act and Film Censorship Act 2002

PP v Chang Ye Siong [2019]

Chang, 35, a restaurant cook was accused of sending a threatening message to a lady that he would disseminate her obscene video to her family members. The video was recorded by Chang during a video call between him and the lady on September 2017. He was also accused of having in his two mobile phones obscene videos on 19 December 2018.

Charges:

Section 503 Penal Code.

Section 292 Penal Code.

Chang pleaded guilty to all charges.

Decision of Petaling Jaya Magistrate Court (01/07/2019):

RM12,000 fine.

PP v Chow Mun Fai [2019]

Chow Mun Fai, a hawker was accused of inciting racial tension between Malays and non-Malays by insulting the death of fire fighter Muhammad Adib Mohd Kassim on Twitter using the profile name of "Alvin@Alvin15358333" on 13 February 2019. He was also accused of uploading an image insulting Prophet Muhammad, which may incite disharmony between Muslims and non-Muslims on 2 March 2019.

He was also accused of posting other offensive tweets using the same profile.

Muhammad Adib died on 17 December 2018 after being admitted to the National Heart Institute due to severe injuries sustained during a riot near Maha Mariamman Temple in Seafield on 26 November 2018.

Charges:

Section 505 Penal Code.

Section 298A(1)(a) Penal Code (3 charges).

Section 233(2) CMA (4 charges).

(pleaded guilty to all charges).

Decision of Kuala Lumpur Sessions Court (06/08/2019):

7 to 30 months imprisonment for all the charges.

PP v Alister Cogia [2019]

Alister, 22, was accused of posting an offensive statement against Islam and Prophet Muhammad on Facebook, using the profile name of "Ayea Yea" on 9, 10, 14 and 24 February 2019.

Charges:

Section 298A(1)(a) Penal Code (5 charges).

Section 233(1)(a) CMA (5 charges).

Decision of Kuala Lumpur Sessions Court (10/03/2019):

1 year imprisonment for each charge.

RM50,000 fine.

PP v Ong Siew Khong [2018]

Ong, 38, a restaurant cook was accused of having in his mobile phone a nude video of his workmate, whom he earlier recorded when she was bathing in their house, on 21 October 2018.

Charges:

Section 292 Penal Code.

Section 14 Minor Offences Act 1955 (pleaded guilty to all charges).

Decision of Petaling Jaya Magistrate Court (30/11/2018):

RM7000 fine for the first charge.

RM100 fine for the second charge.

PP v Zahari Alwi [2018]

Zahari, 56, the caretaker of a children welfare home was accused of intimidating a 10 years old child by opening the door to the bathroom in the welfare home when the victim was inside it in December 2015. He was also accused of having in his laptop an obscene video of the victim in January 2018.

Charges:

Section 509 Penal Code.

Section 5(1) Film Censorship Act.

Zahari pleaded guilty to all charges.

Decision of Ampang Magistrate Court (27/09/2018):

15 months imprisonment for the first charge.

13 months imprisonment for the second charge.

| **PP v Khalid Mohd Ismath [2018]** |

Khalid, 25, an activist was accused of posting 3 separate seditious comments against the Johor royal family, to show solidarity to Kamal Hisham Ja'afar, the ex-lawyer of the Johor royal family. He was also accused of posting offensive comments against the royal family on Facebook from 2 September to 5 October 2015.

Charges:

Section 4(1)(c) Sedition Act (3 charges).

Section 233(1)(a) CMA (11 charges).

Decision of Johor Baharu Sessions Court (29/8/2018):

Discharged and acquitted Khalid after the prosecution withdrew the charges against him.

PP v Ong Hock Soon [2018]

Ong, 40, a salesperson was accused of having in his mobile phone a video of a man defecating. He was also accused of recording the said video when the victim was in a public toilet in a shopping mall. The acts were committed on 13 January 2017.

Charges:

Section 292 Penal Code.

Section 509 Penal Code.

Ong pleaded guilty to all charges.

Decision of Miri Magistrate Court (17/04/2018):

RM3000 for the first charge.

RM4000 for the second charge.

| **Tan Jye Yee and Satu Lagi lwn. PP [2013] 1 LNS 1244 (HC)** |
| **Tan Jye Yee and Anor v PP [2014] 6 MLJ 609 (C0A)** |
| **PP v Tan Jye Yee and Anor [2016]; Lee May Ling v PP [2018] 10 CLJ 742** |

Tan Jye Yee (Alvin Tan) and Lee May Ling (Vivian Lee), 27, were accused of insulting Islam when they uploaded their photo enjoying a dish with the caption "Selamat Berbuka Puasa (with Bak Kut Teh...fragrant, delicious and appetising)" and Halal logo on their Facebook page on 13 July 2013.

They were also accused of posting obscene photos on *http://alviviswingers.tumblr.com* on 6 to 7 July 2013.

Charges:

Section 4(1)(c) Sedition Act.

Section 298A(1)(a) Penal Code.

Section 5(1) Film Censorship Act.

Alvin and Vivian applied to the High Court to quash the charge under section 298A(1)(a) Penal Code, but the High Court dismissed the application on 21 November 2013.

An appeal was filed to the Court of Appeal, and the Court on 10 April 2014 allowed the appeal and ordered the charge to be quashed.

Decision of Kuala Lumpur Sessions Court:

14/04/2016: Discharged and acquitted the accused from the charge under Section 5(1) Film Censorship Act since there was no prima facie case.

27/05/2016: 5 months and 22 days imprisonment for the charge under Section 4(1)(c) Sedition Act.

Vivian had to serve only 8 days in prison since the Court agreed with her lawyer to take into account the number of days she was in remand. The Court allowed a stay of the sentence since Vivian had filed an appeal to the High Court.

Decision of Kuala Lumpur High Court (10/04/2018):

Court allowed the appeal and substituted the sentence with RM5000 fine.

Alvin was sentenced in absentia since he sought asylum in the United States.

| **PP v Nik Adid Nik Mat [2016]** |
| **Nik Adib bin Nik Mat v Public Prosecutor [2017] MLJU 1831** |

Nik Adid, 43, a teacher at a secondary religious school was accused of uploading obscene and false photos entitled "Pesta Bogel" (photos of a group of 12 naked boys with their faces superimposed with the faces of the Primes Minister and leaders of the National Front Party of Malaysia) on *https://www.facebook.com/kopi.rajaakar* on 8 August 2014.

He also had in his possession obscene films and materials promoting obscene films at the same address at 4.45 a.m., 21 August 2014.

Charges:

Section 233(1)(a) CMA.

Section 5(1)(a) Film Censorship Act.

Decision of Kota Bharu Sessions Court (20/07/2016):

1 year imprisonment for each charge.

The sentences were ordered to run consecutively.

Accused appealed to the High Court.

Decision of Kota Bharu High Court (16/11/2017):

Court allowed the appeal and substituted the sentence with:

1 week imprisonment and a RM3000 fine for the first charge.

RM10,000 fine for the second charge.

PP v Muhammad Nor Aliff Basir [2017]

Aliff, 27, was accused of creating and sending an obscene video via WhatsApp with the intent to threaten a 24-year-old man (whom he earlier befriended on WeChat) on April 6, 2017.

He extorted the victim by asking for RM1000 and would distribute his obscene video with the victim if the victim does not pay him the money.

Charge (Magistrate Court):
Section 385 and 292 Penal Code (pleaded guilty).

Charge (Sessions Court):
Section 233(1)(a) CMA (pleaded guilty).

Decision of Ampang Magistrate Court (10/04/2017)
RM5000 fine (extortion under Section 385 Penal Code).
RM3000 fine (possession of obscene material under Section 292 Penal Code).

Decision of Ampang Sessions Court (10/04/2017)
3 months imprisonment and RM15,000 fine (communication of obscene content under the CMA).

PP v Hassan Karim [2016]

Hassan, a politician was accused of posting a seditious statement on Twitter@Hakarim51 on 15 August 2014 and on Twitter@zunarkartunis on 10 February 2016.

He was also accused of alternative charges of using Twitter to post offensive statements on the same dates.

Charges:

Section 4(1)(c) Sedition Act 1948 (2 charges).

Section 233(1)(a) CMA (2 alternative charges).

Decision of Johor Baharu Sessions Court (17/02/2016):

Discharged and acquitted Hassan after the prosecution withdrew the charges against him.

PP v Baderol Sham bin Muhamad Tahir [2015]

Baderol Sham, 37, was accused of uploading obscene content using his account "Putera Katok" on "Kaki3GP Melayu" blog.

Charges:

Section 211 CMA.

Section 292 Penal Code (pleaded guilty to all charges).

Decision of Alor Setar Sessions Court (21/06/2015):

RM4000 fine for the first charge

RM1000 fine and 1 day imprisonment for the second charge.

PP v Tan Keng Hong [2014]

Tan Keng Hong, 32, a car dealer was accused of insulting Melaka traffic police officers on Facebook by calling them "monyet" (monkey) on 25 September 2014. He also initiated communication via Facebook with the intention of harassing them on the same date.

Charges:

Section 504 Penal Code.

Section 233(1)(B) CMA (pleaded guilty to all charges).

Decision of Ayer Keroh Magistrate Court (21/11/2014):

RM3500 fine for the first charge.

RM7000 fine for the second charge.

PP v Chow Mun Fai [2014]

Chow Mun Fai, 36, a site supervisor was accused of posting comments which insulted the month of Ramadan and Eid celebration on his Facebook page "Chow Jack".

Charge:

Section 4(1)(c) Sedition Act 1948.

Section 233(1) CMA (Alternative charge) (pleaded guilty).

Decision of Kuala Lumpur Sessions Court (09/09/2014:

1 year imprisonment.

PP v Mohd Hidayat Abd Ghani @ Mokhtar [2014]

Hidayat, 24, a private university graduate was accused of having in his possession a lady's nude photo and threating to post it online unless she gave him her gold bracelet and necklace, and paid him RM5000 between August to September 2013.

Charges:

Section 384 Penal Code.

Section 385 Penal Code.

Section 292 Penal Code.

Decision of Ayer Keroh Magistrate Court (08/01/2014):

RM8000 fine.

PP v Chan Hon Keong and Anor [2012] 5 LNS 184

Chan Hon Keong, 26, an engineer and his wife, Khoo Hui Shuang, 27, were accused of uploading obscene comments which insulted the Sultan of Perak on the Guestbook at *http://books.dreambook.com/duli/duli.html* which was linked to the Sultan's Office Website i.e. *http://sultan.perak.gov.my* on 13 February 2009.

Charges:

Section 292(a) Penal Code.

Section 233(1)(a) CMA (Alternative charge).

Decision of Butterworth Sessions Court:

Discharged Khoo since there was no prima facie case.

01/06/2012: 1 years imprisonment and RM50,000 fine on Chan under the alternative charge.

Chan appealed against imprisonment, and the Court of Appeal on 7 January 2015 allowed the appeal.

PP v Muhamad Shukri Kassim [2011]

Shukri, 20, an internet cafe cashier was accused of sending a threatening message to a lady that he would disseminate her nude photo on Facebook on 15 June 2011. The photo was earlier sent by the lady to Shukri's mobile phone.

Shukri was also accused of having possession in his mobile phone obscene photos and videos on 16 June 2011.

Charges:

Section 503 Penal Code.

Section 292 Penal Code.

Shukri pleaded guilty to all charges.

Decision of Kuala Lumpur Magistrate Court (07/09/2011):

11 months imprisonment.

RM2500 fine.

PP v Mazlan Majair [2011]

Mazlan, 37, a factory worker was accused of sending two obscene messages via SMS to a housewife on 4 June 2011.

Charges:

Section 14 Minor Offences Act 1955 (2 charges)(pleaded guilty).

Decision of Kuala Lumpur Magistrate Court (09/06/2011):

RM100 fine for each charge.

PP v Johnny Yee Chi Khien [2011]

Johnny, 30, a DVD shop owner was accused of having in his computer hard disk 34 obscene videos on 2 November 2010. He was also accused of having in another computer hard disk 74 obscene videos on the same date.

He was also accused of having in his possession a total of 484 uncertified films in DVDs and having in display 188 uncertified films in DVDs.

Charges:

Section 5(1)(a) Film Censorship Act (2 charges).
Section 6(1)(a) Film Censorship Act (3 charges).

Johnny pleaded guilty to all charges.

Decision of Kota Kinabalu Magistrate Court (05/01/2011):

RM11,000 fine for the first charge.

RM12,000 fine for the second charge.

RM6000 fine for the third charge.

RM6000 fine for the fourth charge.

RM2000 fine for the fifth charge.

PP v Shahrom Mahadi [2010]

Shahrom, 45, a security guard was accused of uploading his nude videos having sex with other guys for the purpose of advertising for his sex service on *sayamahusex.blogspot.com, gambarabangaim.blogspot.com, www.geocities.com/vcdgaymelayu.*

Charges:

Section 292 Penal Code (6 charges).

Section 233(1)(a)(i) CMA (6 alternative charges) (pleaded guilty).

The prosecution then withdrew all charges under section 292.

Decision of Kuala Lumpur Sessions Court (05/06/2010):

6 months imprisonment for each charge under section 233(1)(a)(i)

Offences under the Anti-Fake News Act 2018

PP v Salah Salem Saleh Sulaiman [2018]

Salah, 46, a Denmark citizen working as a horse groomer in Malaysia, was accused of posting false news on YouTube against the police after a Palestinian lecturer was shot to death. The 1 minute and 49 seconds video, posted on 21 April 2018, contained an allegation by Salah that he was with the victim at the murder scene, and it took the police and the ambulance respectively 50 minutes and 1 hour to arrive at the scene.

Charge:

Section 4(1) Anti-Fake News Act (pleaded guilty).

Decision Kuala Lumpur Sessions Court (30/04/2018):

1 week imprisonment (calculated from the date of arrest).

RM10,000 fine.

*Salah was the first person charged & convicted under the Anti Fake News Act 2018 which came into force on 11 April 2018. A Bill to repeal the Act was passed in the House of Representative on 16 August 2018, but the Bill could not be enforced as law since it was voted against by the Senate on 12 September 2018.

Offences under the Official Secrets Act 1972

PP v Subbarau @ Kamalanathan [2015]
PP v Subbarau @ Kamalanathan [2016]
PP v Subbarau @ Kamalanathan [2017]
PP v Subbarau @ Kamalanathan [2018]
Subbarau @ Kamalanathan v PP [2019]

Subbarau, 36, a school teacher was accused of having possession in his mobile phone images of leaked 2014 primary Year 6 examination (UPSR) papers between 8 and 16 September 2014 when the examination was in progress. The images were forwarded to him via WhatsApp.

Charges:

Section 8 Official Secrets Act 1972 (5 charges).

Decision of Seremban Sessions Court (16/04/2015):

Discharged and acquitted Subbarau since there was no prima facie case.

The prosecution appealed against the decision of the court.

Decision of Seremban High Court (05/09/2106):

Dismissed the appeal of the prosecution and retained the decision of the Sessions Court.

The prosecution further appealed to the Court of Appeal.

Decision of the Court of Appeal (25 May 2017):

Ordered Subbarau to enter defence in the Sessions Court on grounds that the prosecution had established a prima facie case.

Decision of Seremban Sessions Court (03/02/2018):

5 years imprisonment for each charge.

Subbarau appealed against his conviction to the High Court.

Decision of Kuala Lumpur High Court (20/02/2019):

Allowed the appeal.

PP v Anparasu A/L Kadampiah [2017]
PP v Anparasu A/L Kadampiah [2017] (HC)
PP v Anparasu A/L Kadampiah [2018]

Anparasu, a school teacher was accused of having possession in his mobile phone images of several pages of leaked 2014 primary Year 6 examination (UPSR) Mathematic and Science papers between 9 and 10 September 2014 when the examination was in progress. The images were forwarded to him via WhatsApp.

Charges:

Section 8 Official Secrets Act 1972 (3 charges).

Decision of Kuala Kangsar Sessions Court (18/01/2017):

Discharged and acquitted Anparasu after the prosecution failed to prove the case prima facie.

The prosecution appealed against the decision of the court.

Decision of Taiping High Court:

Allowed the appeal by the prosecution, and remitted the case to the Sessions Court.

Decision of Kuala Kangsar Sessions Court (06/07/2018):

Acquitted Anparasu since the prosecution failed to prove the case beyond reasonable doubt.

PP v Uma Mageswari A/P Periasamy @ Mayandy [2016]
PP v Uma Mageswari A/P Periasamy @ Mayandy [2017]
PP v Uma Mageswari A/P Periasamy @ Mayandy [2018]

Uma, 27, a school teacher was accused of having possession in her mobile phone images of several pages of leaked 2014 primary Year 6 examination (UPSR) Science papers on 10 September 2014 when the examination was in progress. The images were forwarded to her via WhatsApp.

Charge:
Section 8 Official Secrets Act 1972.

Decision of Kuala Kangsar Sessions Court (28/07/2016):
Discharged and acquitted Uma after the prosecution failed to prove the case prima facie.

The prosecution appealed against the decision of the court.

Decision of Taiping High Court (27/10/2017):
Allowed the appeal by the prosecution, and remitted the case to the Sessions Court.

Decision of Kuala Kangsar Sessions Court (06/04/2018):
Acquitted Uma since the prosecution failed to prove the case beyond reasonable doubt.

CONCLUSION

There are numerous complaints received by the Royal Malaysian Police, Cybersecurity Malaysia and the Communications and Multimedia Commission on cybercrimes but they are not necessarily classified as cybercrimes and they do not end up with prosecution. In the meantime, there are cybercrime cases still pending in the lower courts.

It is the author's hope to provide further information on these cases to the public when the judgements are later passed by the courts.

APPENDIX

COMPUTER CRIMES ACT 1997

Section 2. Interpretation

(1) In this Act, unless the context otherwise requires--

"computer"

means an" electronic, magnetic, optical, electrochemical, or other data processing device, or a group of such interconnected or related devices, performing logical, arithmetic, storage and display functions, and includes any data storage facility or communications facility directly related to or operating in conjunction with such device or group of such interconnected or related devices, but does not include an automated typewriter or typesetter, or a portable hand held calculator or other similar device which is non-programmable or which does not contain any data storage facility;

(Section 3 of the Evidence Act 1950 also provides the same interpretation)

Section 3. Unauthorized access to computer material

(1) A person shall be guilty of an offence if--

    (a) he causes a computer to perform any function with intent to secure access to any program or data held in any computer;

    (b) the access he intends to secure is unauthorized; and

    (c) he knows at the time when he causes the computer to perform the function that is the case.

(2) The intent a person has to have to commit an offence under this section need not be directed at--

    (a) any particular program or data;

    (b) a program or data of any particular kind; or

197

(c) a program or data held in any particular computer.

(3) A person guilty of an offence under this section shall on conviction be liable to a fine not exceeding fifty thousand ringgit or to imprisonment for a term not exceeding five years or to both.

Section 4. Unauthorized access with intent to commit or facilitate commission of further offence

(1) A person shall be guilty of an offence under this section if he commits an offence referred to in section 3 with intent--

(a) to commit an offence involving fraud or dishonesty or which causes injury as defined in the Penal Code [*Act 574*]; or

(b) to facilitate the commission of such an offence whether by himself or by any other person.

(2) For the purposes of this section, it is immaterial whether the offence to which this section applies is to be committed at the same time when the unauthorized access is secured or on any future occasion.

(3) A person guilty of an offence under this section shall on conviction be liable to a fine not exceeding one hundred and fifty thousand ringgit or to imprisonment for a term not exceeding ten years or to both.

Section 5. Unauthorized modification of the contents of any computer

(1) A person shall be guilty of an offence if he does any act which he knows will cause unauthorized modification of the contents of any computer.

(2) For the purposes of this section, it is immaterial that the act in question is not directed at--

(a) any particular program or data;

(b) a program or data of any kind; or

(c) a program or data held in any particular computer.

(3) For the purposes of this section, it is immaterial whether an unauthorized modification is, or is intended to be, permanent or merely temporary.

(4) A person guilty of an offence under this section shall on conviction be liable to a fine not exceeding one hundred thousand ringgit or to imprisonment for a term not exceeding seven years or to both; or be liable to a fine not exceeding one hundred and fifty thousand ringgit or to imprisonment for a term not exceeding ten years or to both, if the act is done with the intention of causing injury as defined in the Penal Code.

COMMUNICATION AND MULTIMEDIA ACT 1998

Section 211. Prohibition on provision of offensive content

(1) No content applications service provider, or other person using a content applications service, shall provide content which is indecent, obscene, false, menacing, or offensive in character with intent to annoy, abuse, threaten or harass any person.

(2) A person who contravenes subsection (1) commits an offence and shall, on conviction, be liable to a fine not exceeding fifty thousand ringgit or to imprisonment for a term not exceeding one year or to both and shall also be liable to a further fine of one thousand ringgit for every day or part of a day during which the offence is continued after conviction.

Section 233. Improper use of network facilities or network service, etc.

(1) A person who--

    (a) by means of any network facilities or network service or applications service knowingly--

        (i)   makes, creates or solicits; and

        (ii)   initiates the transmission of,

        any comment, request, suggestion or other communication which is obscene, indecent, false, menacing or offensive in character with intent to annoy, abuse, threaten or harass another person; or

    (b) initiates a communication using any applications service, whether continuously, repeatedly or otherwise, during which communication may or may not ensue, with or without disclosing his identity and with intent to annoy, abuse, threaten or harass any person at any number or electronic address,

commits an offence.

(2) A person who knowingly--

    (a) by means of a network service or applications service provides any obscene communication for commercial purposes to any person; or

    (b) permits a network service or applications service under the person's control to be used for an activity described in paragraph (a),

commits an offence.

(3) A person who commits an offence under this section shall, on conviction, be liable to a fine not exceeding fifty thousand ringgit or to imprisonment for a term not exceeding one year or to both and shall also be liable to a further fine of one thousand ringgit for every day during which the offence is continued after conviction.

Section 239. Unlawful use, possession or supply of non-standard equipment or device

(1) A person who--

    (a) uses any non-standard equipment or device;

    (b) has in his possession any non-standard equipment or device that he knows or has reason to believe is a non-standard equipment or device for the purpose of installing, working, operating or using the equipment or device; or

    (c) offers for supply, supplies or has in his possession with a view to supply any such non-standard equipment or device,

    commits an offence and shall, on conviction, be liable to a fine not exceeding one hundred thousand ringgit or to imprisonment for a term not exceeding two years or to both.

(2) For the purposes of paragraph (1)(b), a person is deemed to have a non-standard equipment or device in his possession for the purpose of installing, working, operating or using it if it is in his possession, otherwise than for the purpose of supply to another person, and can be operated by doing any of the following:

    (a) connecting the equipment or device to an electric power supply by means of an electric plug or other electric connection;

    (b) switching on the equipment or device;

    (c) connecting a microphone to the equipment or device by inserting a microphone plug into the equipment or device;

    (d) switching on any other thing relevant to the operation of the equipment or device;

    (e) adjusting settings by manipulating the external switches, dials or other controls of the equipment or device; or

    (f) connecting the equipment or device to an antenna.

(3) In any proceedings under this Act, any document purporting to be a certificate given by an authorized officer certifying that any particular equipment or device is a non-standard equipment or device shall be admissible as a prima facie evidence of the facts stated in it until the contrary is proved.

Section 244. Offences by body corporate

(1) If a body corporate commits an offence under this Act or its subsidiary legislation a person who at the time of the commission of the offence was a director, chief executive officer, manager, secretary or other similar officer of the body corporate or was purporting to act in any such capacity or was in any manner or to any extent responsible for the management of any of the affairs of the body corporate or was assisting in such management--

    (a) may be charged severally or jointly in the same proceedings with the body corporate; and

    (b) if the body corporate is found guilty of the offence, shall be deemed to be guilty of that offence unless, having regard to the nature of his functions in that capacity and to all circumstances, he proves--

    (i) that the offence was committed without his knowledge, consent or connivance; and

    (ii) that he had taken all reasonable precautions and exercised due diligence to prevent the commission of the offence.

(2) If any person would be liable under this Act to any punishment or penalty for his act, omission, neglect or default, he shall be liable to the same punishment or penalty for every such act, omission, neglect or

default of any employee or agent of his, or of the employee of the agent, if the act, omission, neglect or default was committed--

(a) by that person's employee in the course of his employment;

(b) by the agent when acting on behalf of that person; or

(c) by the employee of the agent in the course of his employment by the agent or otherwise on behalf of the agent acting on behalf of that person.

PENAL CODE

Section 130C. Committing terrorist acts

(1) Whoever, by any means, directly or indirectly, commits a terrorist act shall be punished—

(a) if the act results in death, with death; and

(b) in any other case, with imprisonment for a term of not less than seven years but not exceeding thirty years, and shall also be liable to fine.

(2) Where in any criminal proceeding it is necessary to decide whether any item or substance is a weapon, a hazardous, radioactive or harmful substance, a toxic chemical or a microbial or other biological agent or toxin, a certificate purporting to be signed by an appropriate authority to the effect that the item or substance described in the certificate is a weapon, a hazardous, radioactive or harmful substance, a toxic chemical or a microbial or other biological agent or toxin shall be sufficient evidence of the facts stated in it.

Section 130FA. Receiving training and instruction from terrorist groups and persons committing terrorist acts

Whoever receives training or instruction, or agrees or arranges to receive training or instruction—

(a) in the making or use of any explosive or other lethal device;

(b) in carrying out a terrorist act; or

(c) in the practice of military exercises or movements,

from a member of a terrorist group or a person engaging in, or preparing to engage in, the commission of a terrorist act shall be punished with imprisonment for a term which may extend to thirty years, and shall also be liable to fine.

130FB. Attendance at place used for terrorist training

(1) Whoever attends at any place, within or outside Malaysia—

(a) knowing or having reason to believe that instruction or training is being provided there wholly or partly for the purposes connected with the commission or preparation of a terrorist act; or

(b) where he could not reasonably have failed to understand that instruction or training was being provided there wholly or partly for such purposes,

shall be punished with imprisonment for a term which may extend to ten years, or with fine.

(2) For the purposes of this section, it shall be irrelevant—

(a) whether the person concerned receives the instruction or training himself; and

(b) whether the instruction or training is provided for purposes connected with one or more particular terrorist act.

(3) References in this section to instruction or training being provided include references to instruction or training being made available.

Section 130G. Inciting, promoting or soliciting property for the commission of terrorist acts

Whoever knowingly—

(a) incites or promotes the commission of a terrorist act;

(b) incites or promotes membership in a terrorist group; or

(c) solicits property for the benefit of a terrorist group or for the commission of a terrorist act,

shall be punished with imprisonment for a term which may extend to thirty years, and shall also be liable to fine.

Section 130J. Soliciting or giving support to terrorist groups or for the commission of terrorist acts

(1) Whoever knowingly and in any manner solicits support for, or gives support to—

(a) any terrorist group; or

(b) the commission of a terrorist act,

shall be punished with imprisonment for life or imprisonment for a term not exceeding thirty years, or with fine, and shall also be liable to forfeiture of any property used or intended to be used in connection with the commission of the offence.

(2) For the purposes of subsection (1), "support" includes—

(a) an offer to provide, or the provision of, forged or falsified travel documents to a member of a terrorist group;

(b) an offer to provide, or the provision of, a skill or an expertise for the benefit of, at the direction of or in association with a terrorist group;

(c) entering or remaining in any country for the benefit of, or at the direction of or in association with a terrorist group;

(d) becoming a member of or professing membership of a terrorist group;

(e) arranging, managing or assisting in arranging or managing a meeting to further the activities of a terrorist group;

(f) using or possessing property for the purpose of committing or facilitating the commission of a terrorist act;

(g) accumulating, stockpiling or otherwise keeping firearms, explosives, ammunition, poisons or weapons to further the activities of a terrorist group;

(h) arranging, managing or assisting in arranging or managing the transportation of persons to further the activities of a terrorist group;

(i) travelling to, entering or remaining in any foreign country to further the activities of a terrorist group or to commit a terrorist act;

(j) encouraging or inducing any person to leave Malaysia to further the activities of a terrorist group or to commit a terrorist act; or

(k) using social media or any other means to—

(i) advocate for or to promote a terrorist group, support for a terrorist group or the commission of a terrorist act; or

(ii) further or facilitate the activities of a terrorist group.

Section 130JB. Possession, etc. of items associated with terrorist groups or terrorist acts.

(1) Whoever—

(a) has possession, custody or control of; or

(b) provides, displays, distributes or sells,

any item associated with any terrorist group or the commission of a terrorist act shall be punished with imprisonment for a term not exceeding seven years, or with fine, and shall also be liable to forfeiture of any such item.

(2) In this section—

"item" includes publications, visual recordings, flags, banners, emblems, insignia and any other thing displaying symbols associated with a terrorist group, terrorist act or ideology of a terrorist group;

"publications" includes all written, pictorial or printed matter, and everything of a nature similar to written or printed matter, whether or not containing any visible representation, or by its form, shape or in any other manner capable of suggesting words or ideas, or an audio recording and every copy, translation and reproduction or substantial translation or reproduction in part or in whole thereof.

Section 130M. Intentional omission to give information relating to terrorist acts

Whoever knowing or having reason to believe that any offence punishable under sections 130C to 130L has been or will be committed intentionally omits to give any information respecting that offence, which he is legally bound to give, shall be punished with imprisonment for a term which may extend to seven years or with fine or with both.

Section 130N. Providing or collecting property for terrorist acts

Whoever, by any means, directly or indirectly, provides or collects or makes available any property intending, knowing or having reasonable grounds to believe that the property will be used, in whole or in part, to commit a terrorist act shall be punished—

(a) if the act results in death, with death; and

(b) in any other case, with imprisonment for a term of not less than seven years but not exceeding thirty years, and shall also be liable to fine,

and shall also be liable to forfeiture of any property so provided or collected or made available.

Section 130Q. Dealing with terrorist property

(1) Whoever knowingly deals, directly or indirectly, in any terrorist property shall be punished with imprisonment for a term which may extend to twenty years, or with fine and shall also be liable to forfeiture of any property so dealt with.

(2) For the purposes of subsection (1), "deals in" includes--

   (a) acquiring or possessing any terrorist property;

   (b) entering into or facilitating, directly or indirectly, any transaction in respect of terrorist property;

   (c) converting, concealing or disguising terrorist property; or

   (d) providing any financial or other services in respect of any terrorist property to or for the benefit of, or at the direction or order of, any terrorist, terrorist entity or terrorist group.

Section 161. Public servant taking a gratification, other than legal remuneration, in respect of an official act

Whoever, being or expecting to be a public servant, accepts or obtains, or agrees to accept or attempts to obtain, from any person, for himself or for any other person, any gratification whatever, other than legal remuneration, as a motive or reward for doing or forbearing to do any official act, or for showing or forbearing to show, in the exercise of his official functions, favour or disfavour to any person, or for rendering or attempting to render any service or disservice to any person, with the Government, or with any member of the Cabinet or of Parliament or of a State Executive Council or Legislative Assembly, or with any public servant, as such, shall be punished with imprisonment for a term which may extend to three years, or with fine, or with both.

Section 292. Sale, etc., of obscene books, etc.

Whoever--

(a) sells, lets to hire, distributes, publicly exhibits or in any manner puts into circulation, or for purposes of sale, hire, distribution, public exhibition or circulation makes, produces or has in his possession any obscene book, pamphlet, paper, drawing, painting representation or figure or any other obscene object whatsoever;

(b) imports, exports or conveys any obscene object for any of the purposes aforesaid, or knowing or having reason to believe that such object will be sold, let to hire, distributed or publicly exhibited or in any manner put into circulation;

(c) takes part in or receives profits from any business in the course of which he knows or has reason to believe that any such obscene objects are for any of the purposes aforesaid, made, produced, purchased, kept, imported, exported, conveyed, publicly exhibited or in any manner put into circulation;

(d) advertises or makes known by any means whatsoever that any person is engaged or is ready to engage in any act which is an offence under this section, or that any such obscene object can be procured from or through any person; or

(e) offers, or attempts to do any act which is an offence under this section,

(f) shall be punished with imprisonment for a term which may extend to three years, or with fine, or with both.

Exception-- This section does not extend to any book, pamphlet, writing, drawing, or painting kept or used *bona fide* for religious purposes or any representation sculptured, engraved, painted or otherwise represented on or in any temple, or on any car used for the conveyance of idols, or kept or used for any religious purpose.

Section 298A. Causing, etc., disharmony, disunity, or feelings of enmity, hatred or ill-will, or prejudicing, etc., the maintenance of harmony or unity, on grounds of religion

(1) Whoever by words, either spoken or written, or by signs, or by visible representations, or by any act, activity or conduct, or by organizing, promoting or arranging, or assisting in organizing, promoting or arranging, any activity, or otherwise in any other manner--

(a) causes, or attempts to cause, or is likely to cause disharmony, disunity, or feelings of enmity, hatred or ill-will; or

(b) prejudices, or attempts to prejudice, or is likely to prejudice, the maintenance of harmony or unity, on grounds of religion, between persons or groups of persons professing the same or different religions, shall be punished with imprisonment for a term of not less than two years and not more than five years.

(2) Sections 173a and 294 of the Criminal Procedure Code shall not apply in respect of an offence under subsection (1).

(3) Where any person alleges or imputes in any manner specified in subsection (1)--

    (a) that any other person, or any class, group or description of persons, professing any particular religion--

        (i)   has ceased to profess that religion;

        (ii)   should not be accepted, or cannot be accepted, as professing that religion; or

        (iii)   does not believe, follow, profess, or belong to, that religion; or

    (b) that anything lawfully done by any religious official appointed, or by any religious authority established, constituted or appointed, by or under any written law, in the exercise of any power, or in the discharge of any duty, or in the performance of any function, of a religious character, by virtue of being so appointed, established or constituted, is not acceptable to such person, or should not be accepted by any other person or persons, or does not accord with or fulfil the requirements of that religion, or is otherwise wrong or improper,

he shall be presumed to have contravened the provisions of subsection (1) by having acted in a manner likely to cause disharmony, disunity or feelings of enmity, hatred or ill-will, or likely to prejudice the maintenance of harmony or unity, between persons or groups of persons professing the religion referred to in the allegation or imputation.

(4)

(a) Where, on any ground of a religious character, any person professing any particular religion uses for burial or cremation of any human corpse a place other than one which is lawfully used for such purpose by persons professing that religion, he shall be presumed to have contravened the provisions of subsection (1) by having acted in a manner likely to cause disharmony, disunity or feelings of enmity, hatred or ill-will, or likely to prejudice the maintenance of harmony or unity, between persons or groups of persons professing that religion.

(b) Where any person, on any ground of a religious character, counsels, advises, instigates, urges, pleads with, or appeals or propagates to, or in any manner or by any means call upon, whether directly or indirectly, any other person or persons professing any particular religion--

   (i)   to use for burial or cremation of any human corpse a place other than one which is lawfully used for such purpose by persons professing that religion;

   (ii)   not to use for burial or cremation of any human corpse any place which is lawfully used for such purpose by persons professing that religion; or

   (iii) not to use for worship any place which is lawfully used for such purpose by persons professing that religion,

he shall be presumed to have contravened the provisions of subsection (1) by having acted in a manner likely to cause disharmony, disunity or feelings of enmity, hatred or ill-will, or likely to prejudice the maintenance of harmony or unity, between persons or groups of persons professing that religion or different religions.

(5) Where any person who is not a religious official appointed, or a religious authority established, constituted or appointed, by or under any written law purports to exercise any power, or to discharge any duty, or to perform any function, of a religious character, being a power, duty or function which can be lawfully exercised, discharged or performed only by a religious official appointed, or a religious authority established, constituted or appointed, by or under any written law, he shall be presumed to have contravened the provisions of subsection (1) by having acted in a manner likely to cause disharmony, disunity or feelings of enmity, hatred or ill-will, or likely to prejudice the maintenance of harmony or unity, between persons or groups of persons professing the same or different religions.

(6) The foregoing provisions of this section shall not apply to--

(a) anything done by any religious authority established, constituted or appointed by or under any written law and conferred by written law with power to give or issue any ruling or decision on any matter pertaining to the religion in respect of which the authority is established, constituted or appointed; or

(b) anything done by any person which is in pursuance of, or which accords with, any ruling or decision given or issued by such religious authority, whether or not such ruling or decision is in writing, and if in writing, whether or not it is published in the *Gazette*.

(7) It shall not be a defence to any charge under this section to assert that what the offender is charged with doing was done in any honest belief in, or in any honest interpretation of, any precept, tenet or teaching of any religion.

(8) If in any proceedings under this section any question arises with regard to the interpretation of any aspect of, or any matter in relation to, any religion, the Court shall accept the interpretation given by any religious authority referred to in subsection(6), being a religious authority in respect of that religion.

Section 378. Theft

Whoever, intending to take dishonestly any movable property out of the possession of any person without that person's consent, moves that property in order to such taking, is said to commit theft.

Explanation 1--A thing so long as it is attached to the earth, not being movable property, is not the subject of theft; but it becomes capable of being the subject of theft as soon as it is severed from the earth.

Explanation 2--A moving, effected by the same act which effects the severance, may be a theft.

Explanation 3--A person is said to cause a thing to move by removing an obstacle which prevented it from moving, or by separating it from any other thing, as well as by actually moving it.

Explanation 4--A person, who by any means causes an animal to move, is said to move that animal, and to move everything which in consequence of the motion so caused is moved by that animal.

Explanation 5--The consent mentioned in the definition may be express or implied, and may be given either by the person in possession, or by any person having for that purpose authority either express or implied.

Section 379. Punishment for theft

Whoever commits theft shall be punished with imprisonment for a term which may extend to seven years, or with fine, or with both, and for a second or subsequent offence shall be punished with imprisonment and shall also be liable to fine or to whipping.

Section 380. Theft in dwelling house, etc.

Whoever commits theft in any building, tent, or vessel, which building, tent, or vessel is used as a human dwelling, or for the custody of property, shall be punished with imprisonment for a term which may extend to ten years, and shall also be liable to fine, and for a second or subsequent offence, shall be punished with imprisonment and shall also be liable to fine or to whipping.

Section 385. Putting person in fear of injury in order to commit extortion

Whoever, in order to commit extortion, puts any person in fear, or attempts to put any person in fear of any injury, shall be punished with imprisonment for a term which may extend to seven years, or with fine, or with whipping or with any two of such punishments.

Section 409. Criminal breach of trust by public servant or agent

Whoever, being in any manner entrusted with property, or with any dominion over property, in his capacity of a public servant or an agent, commits criminal breach of trust in respect of that property, shall be punished with imprisonment for a term which shall not be less than two years and not more than twenty years and with whipping, and shall also be liable to fine.

Section 411. Dishonestly receiving stolen property

Whoever dishonestly receives or retains any stolen property, knowing or having reason to believe the same to be stolen property, shall be punished with imprisonment for a term which may extend to five years or with fine or with both; and if the stolen property is a motor vehicle or any component part of a motor vehicle as defined in section 379A, shall be punished with imprisonment for a term of not less than six months and not more than five years, and shall also be liable to fine.

Section 414. Assisting in concealment of stolen property

Whoever voluntarily assists in concealing or disposing of or making away with property which he knows or has reason to believe to be stolen property, shall be punished with imprisonment for a term which may extend to seven years or with fine or with both; and if the stolen property is a motor vehicle or any component part of a motor vehicle as defined in section 379A, shall be punished with imprisonment for a term of not less than six months and not more than seven years, and shall also be liable to fine.

Section 416. Cheating by personation

A person is said to "cheat by personation" , if he cheats by pretending to be some other person, or by knowingly substituting one person for another, or representing that he or any other person is a person other than he or such other person really is.

Explanation--The offence is committed whether the individual personated is a real or imaginary person.

Section 417. Punishment for cheating

Whoever cheats shall be punished with imprisonment for a term which may extend to five years or with fine, or with both.

Section 420. Cheating and dishonestly inducing delivery of property

Whoever cheats and thereby dishonestly induces the person deceived, whether or not the deception practised was the sole or main inducement, to deliver any property to any person, or to make, alter, or destroy the whole or any part of a valuable security, or anything which is signed or sealed, and which is capable of being converted into a valuable security, shall be punished with imprisonment for a term which shall not be less than one year and not more than ten years and with whipping, and shall also be liable to fine.

Section 424. Dishonest or fraudulent removal or concealment of consideration

Whoever dishonestly or fraudulently conceals or removes any property of himself or any other person, or dishonestly or fraudulently assists in the concealment or removal thereof, or dishonestly releases any demand or claim to which he is entitled, shall be punished with imprisonment for a term which may extend to five years or with fine or with both.

Section 467. Forgery of a valuable security or will

Whoever forges a document which purports to be a valuable security or a will, or an authority to adopt a son, or which purports to give authority to any person to make or transfer any valuable security, or to receive the principal, interest or dividends thereon, or to receive or deliver any money, movable property or valuable security, or any document purporting to be

217

an acquitance or receipt, acknowledging the payment of money, or an acquittance or receipt for the delivery of any movable property or valuable security, shall be punished with imprisonment for a term which may extend to twenty years, and shall also be liable to fine.

Section 471. Using as genuine a forged document

Whoever fraudulently or dishonestly uses as genuine any document which he knows or has reason to believe to be a forged document, shall be punished in the same manner as if he had forged such document.

Section 499. Defamation

Whoever, by words either spoken or intended to be read or by signs, or by visible representations, makes or publishes any imputation concerning any person, intending to harm, or knowing or having reason to believe that such imputation will harm the reputation of such person, is said, except in the cases hereinafter excepted, to defame that person.

Explanation 1-- It may amount to defamation to impute anything to a deceased person, if the imputation would harm the reputation of that person if living, and is intended to be hurtful to the feelings of his family or other near relatives.

Explanation 2-- It may amount to defamation to make an imputation concerning a company, or an association or collection of persons as such.

Explanation 3-- An imputation in the form of an alternative, or expressed ironically, may amount to defamation.

Explanation 4-- No imputation is said to harm a person's reputation, unless that imputation directly or indirectly, in the estimation of others, lowers the moral or intellectual character of that person, or lowers the character of that person in respect of his caste or of his calling, or lowers the credit of that person, or causes it to be believed that the body of that person is in a loathsome state, or in a state generally considered as disgraceful.

First Exception-- It is not defamation to impute anything which is true concerning any person, if it is for the public good that the imputation should be made or published. Whether or not it is for the public good is a question of fact.

Second Exception-- It is not defamation to express in good faith any opinion whatever respecting the conduct of a public servant in the discharge of his public functions, or respecting his character, so far as his character appears in that conduct, and no further.

Third Exception-- It is not defamation to express in good faith any opinion whatever respecting the conduct of any person touching any public question, and respecting his character, so far as his character appears in that conduct, and no further.

Fourth Exception-- It is not defamation to publish a substantially true report of the proceedings of a Court, or of any Legislative Assembly, or of the result of any such proceedings.

Explanation-- A Justice of the Peace or other officer holding an inquiry in open Court preliminary to a trial in a Court, is a Court within the meaning of the above section.

Fifth Exception-- It is not defamation to express in good faith any opinion whatever respecting the merits of any case, civil or criminal, which has been decided by a Court, or respecting the conduct of any person as a party, witness or agent, in any such case, or respecting the character of such person, as far as his character appears in that conduct, and no further.

Section 500. Punishment for defamation

Whoever defames another shall be punished with imprisonment for a term which may extend to two years, or with fine, or with both.

Section 503. Criminal intimidation

Whoever threatens another with any injury to his person, reputation or property, or to the person or reputation of any one in whom that person is interested, with intent to cause alarm to that person, or to cause that person to do any act which he is not legally bound to do, or to omit to do any act which that person is legally entitled to do, as the means of avoiding the execution of such threat, commits criminal intimidation.

Section 504. Intentional insult with intent to provoke a breach of the peace

Whoever intentionally insults, and thereby gives provocation to any person, intending or knowing it to be likely that such provocation will cause him to break the public peace, or to commit any other offence, shall be punished with imprisonment for a term which may extend to two years, or with fine, or with both.

Section 507. Criminal intimidation by an anonymous communication

Whoever commits the offence of criminal intimidation by an anonymous communication, or by having taken precautions to conceal the name or abode of the person from whom the threat comes, shall be punished with imprisonment for a term which may extend to two years, in addition to the punishment provided for the offence by section 506.

Section 509. Word or gesture intended to insult the modesty of a person

Whoever, intending to insult the modesty of any person, utters any word, makes any sound or gesture, or exhibits any object, intending that such word or sound shall be heard, or that such gesture or object shall be seen by such person, or intrudes upon the privacy of such person, shall be punished with imprisonment for a term which may extend to five years, or with fine, or with both.

SEDITION ACT 1948
Section 4. Offences

(1) Any person who--

    (a) does or attempts to do, or makes any preparation to do, or conspires with any person to do, any act which has or which would, if done, have a seditious tendency;

    (b) utters any seditious words;

    (c) prints, publishes, sells, offers for sale, distributes or reproduces any seditious publication; or

    (d) imports any seditious publication,

shall be guilty of an offence and shall, on conviction, be liable for a first offence to a fine not exceeding five thousand ringgit or to imprisonment for a term not exceeding three years or to both, and, for a subsequent offence, to imprisonment for a term not exceeding five years; and any seditious publication found in the possession of the person or used in evidence at his trial shall be forfeited and may be destroyed or otherwise disposed of as the court directs.

(2) Any person who without lawful excuse has in his possession any seditious publication shall be guilty of an offence and shall, on

conviction, be liable for a first offence to a fine not exceeding two thousand ringgit or to imprisonment for a term not exceeding eighteen months or to both, and, for a subsequent offence, to imprisonment for a term not exceeding three years, and the publication shall be forfeited and may be destroyed or otherwise disposed of as the court directs.

The Sedition Act was amended in 2015, and the above provision now reads (amendment in italic):

Section 4. Offences

(1) Any person who--

    (a) does or attempts to do, or makes any preparation to do, or conspires with any person to do, any act which has or which would, if done, have a seditious tendency;

    (b) utters any seditious words;

    (c) prints, publishes or *causes to be published*, sells, offers for sale, distributes or reproduces any seditious publication; or

    (d) *propagates* any seditious publication,

shall be guilty of an offence and shall, on conviction, be liable *to imprisonment for a term of not less than three years but not exceeding seven years*; and any seditious publication found in the possession of the person or used in evidence at his trial shall be forfeited and may be destroyed or otherwise disposed of as the court directs.

(2) Any person who without lawful excuse has in his possession any seditious publication shall be guilty of an offence and shall, on conviction, be liable for a first offence to a fine not exceeding two thousand ringgit or to imprisonment for a term not exceeding eighteen months or to both, and, for a subsequent offence, to imprisonment for a

term not exceeding three years, and the publication shall be forfeited and may be destroyed or otherwise disposed of as the court directs.

(1a) Any person who—

(a) does or attempts to do, or makes any preparation to do, or conspires with any person to do, any act which has or which would, if done, have a seditious tendency;

(b) utters any seditious words;

(c) prints, publishes or causes to be published, sells, offers for sale, distributes or reproduces any seditious publication; or

(d) propagates any seditious publication,

and by such act causes bodily injury or damage to property shall be guilty of an offence and shall, on conviction, be liable to imprisonment for a term of not less than three years but not exceeding twenty years.

FILM CENSORSHIP ACT 2002

Section 5. Obscene film

(1) No person shall—

(a) have or cause himself to have in his possession, custody, control or ownership; or

(b) circulate, exhibit, distribute, display, manufacture, produce, sell or hire,

any film or film-publicity material which is obscene or is otherwise against public decency.

(2) Any person who contravenes subsection (1) commits an offence and shall be liable on conviction to a fine of not less than ten thousand ringgit and not more than fifty thousand ringgit or to imprisonment for a term not exceeding five years or to both.

ANTI-FAKE NEWS ACT 2018

Section 4. Creating, offering, publishing, etc., fake news or publication containing fake news

(1) Any person who, by any means, maliciously creates, offers, publishes, prints, distributes, circulates or disseminates any fake news or publication containing fake news commits an offence and shall, on conviction, be liable to a fine not exceeding five hundred thousand ringgit or to imprisonment for a term not exceeding six years or to both, and in the case of a continuing offence, to a further fine not exceeding three thousand ringgit for every day during which the offence continues after conviction.

(2) The Court may, in addition to any punishment specified in subsection (1), order the person convicted of an offence under that subsection to make an apology to the person affected by the commission of the offence in the manner determined by the Court.

(3) Failure to comply with an order made under subsection (2) shall be punishable as a contempt of court.

OFFICIAL SECRETS ACT 1972

Section 8. Wrongful communication, etc., of official secret

(1) If any person having in his possession or control any official secret or any secret official code word, countersign or password which—

    (a) relates to or is used in a prohibited place or relates to anything in such a place;

    (b) relates to munitions of war and to other apparatus, equipment and machinery which are used in the maintenance of the safety and security of Malaysia;

    (c) has been made or obtained in contravention of this Act;

(d) has been entrusted in confidence to him by any public officer; or

(e) he has made or obtained, or to which he has had access, owing to his position as a person who holds or has held office in the public service, or as a person who holds, or has held a contract made on behalf of the Government, or as a person who is or has been employed by or under a person who holds or has held such an office or contract,

does any of the following:

(a) communicates directly or indirectly any such informationor thing to any foreign country other than any foreign country to which he is duly authorized to communicate it, or any person other than a person to whom he is duly authorized to communicate it or to whom it is his duty to communicate it;

(b) uses any such official secret or thing as aforesaid for the benefit of any foreign country other than any foreign country for whose benefit he is duly authorized to use it, or in any other manner prejudicial to the safety or interests of Malaysia;

(c) retains in his possession or control any such thing as aforesaid when he has no right to retain it, or when it is contrary to his duty to retain it, or fails to comply with all lawful directions issued by lawful authority with regard to the return or disposal thereof; or

(d) fails to take reasonable care of, or so conducts himself as to endanger the safety or secrecy of, any such official secret or thing,

he shall be guilty of an offence punishable with imprisonment for a term not less than one year but not exceeding seven years.

(2) If any person receives any official secret or any secret official code word, countersign or password knowing or having reasonable ground to believe at the time when he receives it, that the official secret, code

word, countersign or password is communicated to him in contravention of this Act, he shall, unless he proves that the communication to him of the official secret, code word, countersign or password was contrary to his desire, be guilty of an offence punishable with imprisonment for a term not less than one year but not exceeding seven years.

ANTI-MONEY LAUNDERING, ANTI-TERRORISM FINANCING AND PROCEEDS OF UNLAWFUL ACTIVITIES 2001

Section 4. Offence of money laundering

(1) Any person who—

    (a) engages, directly or indirectly, in a transaction that involves proceeds of an unlawful activity or instrumentalities of an offence;

    (b) acquires, receives, possesses, disguises, transfers, converts, exchanges, carries, disposes of or uses proceeds of an unlawful activity or instrumentalities of an offence;

    (c) removes from or brings into Malaysia, proceeds of an unlawful activity or instrumentalities of an offence; or

    (d) conceals, disguises or impedes the establishment of the true nature, origin, location, movement, disposition, title of, rights with respect to, or ownership of, proceeds of an unlawful activity or instrumentalities of an offence,

commits a money laundering offence and shall on conviction be liable to imprisonment for a term not exceeding fifteen years and shall also be liable to a fine of not less than five times the sum or value of the proceeds of an unlawful activity or instrumentalities of an offence at the time the offence was committed or five million ringgit, whichever is the higher.

(2) For the purposes of subsection (1), it may be inferred from any objective factual circumstances that—

(a) the person knows, has reason to believe or has reasonable suspicion that the property is the proceeds of an unlawful activity or instrumentalities of an offence; or

(b) the person without reasonable excuse fails to take reasonable steps to ascertain whether or not the property is the proceeds of an unlawful activity or instrumentalities of an offence.

(3) For the purposes of any proceedings under this Act, where the proceeds of an unlawful activity are derived from one or more unlawful activities, such proceeds need not be proven to be from any specific unlawful activity.

(4) A person may be convicted of an offence under subsection (1) irrespective of whether there is a conviction in respect of a serious offence or foreign serious offence or that a prosecution has been initiated for the commission of a serious offence or foreign serious offence.

DIRECT SALES AND ANTI-PYRAMID SCHEME ACT 1993
Section 27B. Unlawful to promote or conduct pyramid scheme

(1) No person shall promote or cause to be promoted a pyramid scheme.

(2) Any person who contravenes subsection (1) shall be guilty of an offence and shall, on conviction, be liable—

(a) where such person is a body corporate, partnership or society, to a fine of not less than one million ringgit and not more than ten million ringgit and, for a second or subsequent offence, to a fine of not less than ten million ringgit and not more than fifty million ringgit;

(b) where such person is not a body corporate, partnership or society, to a fine of not less than five hundred thousand ringgit and not more than five million ringgit or to imprisonment for a term not exceeding five years or to both and, for a second or subsequent offence, to a fine of not less than one million ringgit and not more than ten million ringgit or to imprisonment for a term not exceeding ten years or to both.

(3) Where a person, being a director, manager, secretary or other similar officer of a body corporate, a partner in a partnership or an office-bearer in a society, as the case may be, is guilty of an offence under this section by virtue of section 38, he shall be liable to the penalty provided for under paragraph (2)(b).

www.ingramcontent.com/pod-product-compliance
Lightning Source LLC
Chambersburg PA
CBHW021357210526
45463CB00001B/124